420070

STORIES OF EX-SLAVES
(Texas)

ADELINE CUNNINGHAM, 1210 Florida St.,
born 1852, was a slave in Lavaca County,
4½ miles n. e. of Hallettsville. She
was a slave of Washington Greenlee Foley
and his grandson, John Woods. The Foley
plantation consisted of several square
leagues, each league containing 4,428.4
acres. Adeline is tall, spare and primly
erect, with fiery brown eyes, which ~~~~~
snap~ ~~~~~~~~~~~~~~ when she recalls the
~~~~~~~~~~~~~~~~~ slave days. The house is
somewhat pretentious and well furnished.
The day was hot and the granddaughter prepared ice water for her grandmother and
the interviewer. House and porch were
very clean.

"I was bo'n on ole man Foley's plantation in Lavaca County. He's

got more'n 100 slaves. He always buy slaves and he never sell. How many

acres of lan' he got? Lawd, dat man ain't got acres, he got leagues. Dey

raises cotton and co'n, and cattle and hawgs. Ole man Foley's plantation

run over Lavaca and Colorado county, he got 1600 acres in one block and

some of it on de Navidad River. Ole man Foley live in a big log house wid

two double rooms and a hall, and he build a weavin' house agin his own house

and dey's anudder house wid de spinnin' wheels. And ole man Foley run his

own cotton gin and his own grindin' mill where dey grinds de co'n and dey

got a big potato patch.

"Dey was rough people and dey treat ev'ry body rough. We lives in

de quarter; de houses all jine close togedder but you kin walk 'tween 'em.

All de cabins has one room and mostly two fam'lies bunks togedder in de one

room wid dirt floors. De slaves builds de cabins, de slaves got no money,

dey got no land.

"No suh, we never goes to church. Times we sneaks in de woods and

prays de Lawd to make us free and times one of de slaves got happy and made

a noise dat dey heered at de big house and den de overseer come and whip us

What's that?
You want me to tell
you 'bout slavery
days? . . . Well,
I'll tell you some to
put in your book.
      --Elizabeth Sparks

Lots of old slaves closes
the door before they tell
the truth about their days
of slavery . . .
                    --Martin Jackson

Unchained Memories

READINGS FROM THE SLAVE NARRATIVES

FOREWORD BY

HENRY LOUIS GATES, JR.

INTRODUCTION BY

SPENCER CREW

AND

CYNTHIA GOODMAN

BULFINCH PRESS

AOL TIME WARNER BOOK GROUP

BOSTON • NEW YORK • LONDON

The interviews of Beverly Jones and Ishrael Massie first
appeared in *Weevils in the Wheat: Interviews with
Virginia Ex-Slaves,* by Charles L. Perdue, Jr., Thomas E.
Barden, and Robert K. Phillips, courtesy of the
Hampton University Archives.

The interview of Jack and Rosa Maddox is taken from
American Slave, supp. ser. 2, vol. 7, pp. 2521-50.

Design by Wendy Byrne

First Edition

ISBN 0-8212-2842-0

Library of Congress Control Number 2002113761

Endpapers: Facsimile pages from the *Slave Narratives*
collection in the Library of Congress.

Bulfinch Press is a division of
AOL Time Warner Book Group.

PRINTED IN THE UNITED STATES OF AMERICA

CONTENTS

Foreword

Imagine hundreds of interviewers, white and black, fanning out all over the South at the height of the Great Depression, armed with a list of questions, writing down the testimonies of thousands of aged African Americans about their recollection of their lives under America's "peculiar institution," slavery in the antebellum South, and the whole splendid project funded by the United States government! As incredible as it may sound to us today, this ambitious undertaking did indeed take place in the 1930s, preserving the recollection of ex-slaves in the archive known as the Slave Narrative Collection of the Federal Writers' Project. The collection—consisting of forty-one volumes—was not fully published until the late 1970s, under the masterful editorial direction of the historian George P. Rawick. Rawick's scrupulous editorial standards, coupled with his broad vision, have led to renewed scholarly interest in this massive archive of the testimony of a group of people best able to re-create plantation life and culture from the inside, the slaves themselves. Today, these fascinating interviews are available, indexed by Donald M. Jacobs (Greenwood, 1981).

The historian Norman Yetman, as early as 1967, had established the details of the evolution of this project in an often-cited essay entitled "The Background of the Slave Narrative Collection," published in the journal *American Quarterly*. Subsequent scholarly accounts, such as those by Paul D. Escott (*Slavery Remembered*, 1979), have added important information to Yetman's pioneering work. My own understanding of the history of these narratives is dependent upon the scholarship of Yetman, Escott, and Rawick.

Slave Narratives: A Folk History of Slavery in the United States from Interviews with Former Slaves consists of two thousand three hundred interviews gathered in seventeen states between 1936 and 1938. When the Civil War ended in 1865, the ex-slaves who would be interviewed seventy-odd years later ranged in age from one to over thirty, but most (67 percent) were between six and twenty. As we might expect, and as Yetman reports, "two-thirds were over eighty when interviewed; 'the total sample' represented approximately 2 per cent of the total ex-slave population at the time." This remarkable collection ensured the preservation of the voices and sentiments of far more ex-slaves than had existed before; after all, only about one hundred slave narratives were published by ex-slaves in book form before 1865. While much longer and more detailed than the oral narratives, the written narratives—which today are seen by scholars as the formal foundation of the African-American literary tradition itself—are, by definition, a much more limited sample of slave opinion than the vastly larger interview database. And despite the advanced age of the interviewees, *Slave Narratives* unlocks the secrets of this brutal institution; using the voices of the slaves themselves was the key. WPA interviewers often photographed the former slaves, occasionally with the aid of a photographer. Five hundred of these portraits are housed in the Library of Congress with the narratives, and several of them are reproduced in this book.

Why turn to the slave, so very many years after the abolition of slavery? There are several reasons, but the most important, as Yetman argues, is the emergence of black historians in the first three decades of the twentieth century who were intent upon refuting the rosy—and often racist—depictions of slavery propagated by scholars who were little more than apologists for the Confederacy. Chief among these was the Yale historian Ulrich B. Phillips, whose *American Negro Slavery* (1918) portrayed the slave as happy and content, his treatment by his master generous, "civilizing," and humane. Even many black people accepted these stereotypical notions about the slave experience, urging us to forget about slavery, at best an embarrassing episode in African-American

history. What more effective way to counter these claims than to hear from the ex-slaves themselves?

Charles S. Johnson, the great black sociologist, launched a project at Fisk University in 1929 to interview slaves in Nashville, rural Tennessee, Kentucky, and later in Macon County, Alabama. That same year, the historian John B. Cade at Southern University embarked upon a similar course of interviews. The scholar Lawrence D. Reddick, at Kentucky State College, proposed in 1934 that the Federal Emergency Relief Fund administration systematically interview ex-slaves as part of its program, in part to give jobs to "unemployed Negro college graduates." Reddick had worked with Johnson on his project at Fisk. Reddick's project yielded 250 interviews gathered in Indiana and Kentucky in 1934 and 1935, but it was aborted because of organizational and funding problems.

Under the urging of John A. Lomax, a seminal figure in the collection of American folklore and the honorary curator of the Archives of American Folksong in the Library of Congress, and Sterling A. Brown, a poet, critic, and Howard University professor, who held a master's degree in English from Harvard, and who was named the Director of the Office of Negro Affairs within the Federal Writers' Project, the gathering of the oral narratives of ex-slaves became a reality in the second half of the 1930s. Brown saw to it that blacks gained employment in as many southern states as he could—notably in Virginia, Florida, and Louisiana. Nevertheless, most units of the Federal Writers' Project remained segregated, according to Jim Crow practices of the time.

The collection of the interviews became an official program of the FWP in April 1937, but the Reverend J. C. Wright, a member of the staff of the Atlanta Urban League, had proposed that the Georgia Writers' Project commence such interviews in July 1936. Black and white interviewers, Yetman tells us, gathered over one hundred interviews with former slaves. When Sterling Brown read samples of these early interviews, he called them "colorful and valuable," and encouraged a more sustained effort. A month later, in March 1937, Brown, John Lomax, and George Cronyn, the Associate Director of the Federal Writers' Project, read copies of interviews completed by the Florida Writers' Project, including some done by the great black anthropologist and novelist Zora Neale Hurston, in search of black folklore. Yetman concludes that it was "Lomax [who] was chiefly responsible for the inclusion of this activity as an integral aspect of the FWP program. Excited by the possibilities afforded by the structure and emphases of the Writers' Project for a large-scale collection of the narratives, he proposed that these efforts should be extended on a more systematic basis to the remaining southern

and border states. On April 1, 1937, these activities were formally initiated with the dispatch of instructions to each of these states to direct their workers to the task of interviewing former slaves."

Lomax's office, the Folklore Division of the FWP, directed the project. But Brown's Office of Negro Affairs also took a keen interest, producing Brown's crucial memo to interviewers about the delicacy of transcribing black vernacular English. (See *The Slave's Narrative*, Charles C. Davis and Henry Louis Gates, Jr., eds., Oxford University Press, 1993.) After April 1937, the interviewers were "almost exclusively whites," leading many scholars to wonder if the ex-slaves censored themselves in accounts of the harsher aspects of slave life. The interviews took place "in all the southern states, as well as in New York and Rhode Island." The richest results, Yetman maintains, were found in interviews conducted in Alabama, North Carolina, South Carolina, Texas, and Arkansas. Unfortunately, by early 1939 the project had been terminated. Perhaps the best assessment of the significance of these narratives is that of Benjamin A. Botkin, the well-respected folklorist who succeeded Lomax as Folklore Editor of the Writers' Project. Botkin's *Lay My Burden Down*, a collection of black folklore taken from the interviews, was the first book to emerge from the collection and alerted subsequent generations of scholars to the extraordinarily rich material contained in it. Botkin wrote in 1942: "Beneath all the surface contradiction and exaggerations, the fantasy and flattery, [the narratives] possess an essential truth and humanity which surpasses as it supplements history and literature."

Yetman's conclusion is just as moving: "The Collection today stands as a monument to the former slaves, whose collective testimony surpasses in vividness and freshness many other efforts to reconstruct ante-bellum life. The narratives, above all, illumine the personal reality of slave life."

In 1977 and 1979, Greenwood Press published twenty-two additional volumes of interviews gathered by the historian George P. Rawick from FWP and WPA archives scattered throughout the country, many of which had not been deposited in the Library of Congress when the initial collection of nineteen volumes was donated in 1941. The result is the largest database of the thoughts and feelings of former slaves in the history of slavery—an institution that is old as civilization itself. And nothing will do more to breathe life into these thousands of pages of testimony, pregnant with nuance and implication, than HBO's documentary *Unchained Memories: Readings from the Slave Narratives*. It is as if a section of the lost Library of Alexandria had been rediscovered, filmed, and narrated by many of the greatest actors of our era.

—HENRY LOUIS GATES, JR.

Introduction

Unchained Memories: Readings from the Slave Narratives, the title of this publication, the documentary film produced by HBO for release in February 2003, and an exhibition organized by the National Underground Railroad Freedom Center, Cincinnati, Ohio, for a national museum tour, are all based primarily on a group of oral histories, documents, and photographs housed at the Library of Congress in Washington, D.C. This archival collection, titled "Born in Slavery: Slave Narratives from the Federal Writers' Project, 1936–38," includes more than 2,300 first-person accounts of life as a slave and 500 black-and-white photographs of the former slaves who were interviewed. These materials were gathered in seventeen states primarily during 1937 and early 1938 by the Federal Writers' Project (FWP) of the Works Progress Administration.

The Works Progress Administration, or WPA, was created by President Franklin D. Roosevelt as an executive order and authorized by Congress in 1935. This visionary agency gave gainful employment to those hardest hit by the Great Depression and, in the process, produced many significant works that still benefit us today. These works include dams, such as the Hoover Dam, bridges, highways, public swimming pools, state guidebooks, and works of art, architecture, and oral history.

The original interviews were collected at the state level by field workers, who visited former slaves often several times in an effort to get the maximum amount of reliable information. Sometimes photographs were also taken. Once the interviews were complete, the interviewers turned over their records to the FWP director in their state for editing prior to submission to Washington. Each interview includes the names of the interviewer and the individual who was interviewed, the time and place of the interview, and photographs, when they exist. The interviewing of former slaves was curtailed in 1938, as the uncertain future of these narratives diminished interest in their collection. In addition, several other Federal Writers' Projects needed staffing, and FWP administrators believed not only that additional interviews would be redundant but also that there were not many more ex-slaves to interview. Both beliefs were untrue. The project was terminated in 1939, when the Federal Writers' Project lost its funding. At that time, the Library of Congress requested that all state offices send the manuscripts in their possession to the library for preservation and administration. Although most of the manuscripts made it to the Library of Congress, some ended up in other collections throughout the country.

Fortunately, the Writers' Unit of the Library of Congress Project assumed responsibility for these interviews and other related materials, numbering approximately a thousand documents. Benjamin A. Botkin, folklore editor of the Writers' Project, began assembling and editing the archive in preparation for the publication and microfilming of a seventeen-volume reference work, *Slave Narratives: A Folk History of Slavery in the United States from Interviews with Former Slaves*, which was published in 1941. The narratives are grouped in these volumes by state. Today this vast and invaluable collection along with other related materials are available to the public online.

In addition to the digital archives, the Manuscript Division of the Library of Congress also contains the original handwritten interviews, the subsequent typescripts, approximately two hundred additional photographs that are not part of the bound volumes and unavailable online, and documents including newspaper advertisements of slave auctions, state laws and bills relating to slavery, bills of sale, and "WPA Writers' Program Records Appraisal Sheets." The information on these records, which were compiled at the library, includes the place and date of origin, name of the compiler or field worker, purpose, status of the study, sources, reliability and value of the material, style, suggested revisions and corrections, and correspondence consulted (if applicable).

The massive WPA undertaking was not the first recording of firsthand data on this era from former slaves. The initial gathering of accounts by former slaves was conducted in 1929 by Fisk University in Tennessee, Southern University in Louisiana, and Prairie View State College in Texas. Moreover, the multistate project was not the original assignment for the Writers' Project. Initially, the writers were instructed to document folklore in order to produce state guidebooks by interviewing ordinary people about their lives. In the states of Florida, Georgia, South Carolina, and Virginia, the interviewers took the initiative to focus their research on former slaves.

In our preparation of this publication, we have been extremely fortunate to be able to consult with Stetson Kennedy, former state director, WPA Writers' Project, Folklore, Oral History, and Ethnic Studies, 1937–1942, who currently lives in Jacksonville, Florida. Thanks to Mr. Kennedy's excellent recollections of his experiences and his prodigious efforts to preserve and perpetuate the contributions of the WPA program, we were able to confirm many aspects of our research on the *Slave Narratives*. Kennedy, who later wrote the *Jim Crow Guide The Way It Was*, which was praised and published by Jean Paul Sartre in Paris in 1956, when no one in the United States had the courage to publish it, has won recognition as one of America's great pioneer folklorists. In his informative article, "A Florida Treasure Hunt," also available on the Library of Congress web site, Mr. Kennedy recalls how he and everyone working on the WPA, with the exception of the administrators, "had to sign a Pauper's Oath—that we had no money, no property, and no prospect of getting any of those things." As a student at the University of Florida when he applied, Kennedy easily qualified and was paid $37.50 every two weeks for his services as a "Junior Interviewer."

Mr. Kennedy and his colleagues chose to concentrate their efforts on the former slaves—or "ex-slaves," as Kennedy said they were then called—because of their keen recognition that "there was a window of opportunity that was fast closing." Although a number of people who had been slaves as children or young adults were still alive, they were quite elderly, and their numbers were diminishing rapidly. In fact, the majority of those interviewed were at least eighty years old.

When the documentation on former slaves conducted particularly in Florida and other states came to the attention of John Lomax, then National Adviser on Folklore and Folkways for the FWP in Washington, he issued the directive for systematic interviewing in these states and thirteen others to collect the oral histories. The field workers were given a set of instructions about how to conduct the interviews, what questions they were to ask, and how to capture the dialect of their informants. The narratives presented here are reproduced just as they appear in the original documents. These records are also currently available in the Manuscripts Division of the Library of Congress in Washington, D.C.

Despite the attempts at systematization and impartiality, numerous questions have arisen about the accuracy as well as the means of collecting this information. In evaluating the accuracy of first-person resources, the researcher must keep in mind numerous factors, including the qualifications of both the interviewer and the interviewee as well as the conditions specific not only to the interview itself but also to the sociocultural milieu at the time of the interview. The insensitive tone of the comments of one editor who filled out an Appraisal Sheet in 1941 and refers to a runaway slave's account of his harrowing escape from predatory dogs as "somewhat expanded" is an excellent indication of the racial bias when these narratives were accumulated and reviewed.

It is noteworthy that until the absence of black participants on this project was noted by black leaders, there were no African-American interviewers. Even after an Office of Negro Affairs was formed to correct this situation, and Howard University professor Sterling A. Brown was brought on board to oversee the inclusion of African Americans in the Writers' Project, for all practical purposes in several southern states, African Americans were still not included as interviewers. Furthermore, even in Virginia, Florida, and Louisiana, where the contributions of African Americans were significant, their participation was still limited by the southern mandate that separate units exist for black and white participants. This policy is recorded in one of the documents at the library that includes the name and race of each interviewer.

Furthermore, despite the fact that John Lomax insisted that the interviews not be altered in any way upon transcription, he did not take into account fully the possible effect that having a white person interview a former slave might have upon the interview. In fact, in this era, it is believed that some of the interviewees probably were not as forthcoming to their white interviewers as they might have been had the interviewer also been black. That is, for the benefit of their white interviewer, they may have recounted a somewhat softened depiction of their slave experience.

Matching race of interviewer to race of interviewee was one of Kennedy's responsibilities. He maintained this policy whenever possible because, in his estimation, there are distinct differences visible in the interview styles and results depending on the race of the interviewer. As Kennedy explained the obvious disparities, "Jim Crow was the Editor-in-

Chief, looking over everyone's shoulders, black and white."

The qualifications of the project's staff have also been questioned because of their lack of training as folklorists. Kennedy defends this lack of training, saying, "There wasn't any to be had." And he insists that "since our interviewers were just as folksy as the interviewees, they could knock on almost any door, and the rapport was there."

Although there was a set procedure for conducting the interviews, the interviewers adjusted instructions to fit their own personal interview style. Accurate recording of language was a pervasive problem. Even for those who were familiar with the dialect spoken by the former slaves, capturing the pronunciations was extremely difficult. The recommendation of John Lomax "that truth to idiom be paramount, and exact truth to pronunciation secondary" was not much help to those struggling with how best to record their informants. Concerning the usefulness to the interviewers of the questions prepared in Washington, Mr. Kennedy has wryly commented, "To some extent they were helpful and to some extent not." In fact, the Library of Congress acknowledges the possible limitations with the following disclaimer on the opening page of the "Slave Narratives" web site: "The Library of Congress presents these documents as part of the record of the past. These primary historical documents reflect the attitudes, perspectives, and beliefs of different times. The Library of Congress does not endorse the views expressed in these collections, which may contain materials offensive to some readers."

Yet despite all the disclaimers and inconsistencies, anyone who reads a number of these narratives can glimpse beneath the layer of artifice an unequaled portrayal of the slave era in the United States. This portrayal is powerfully conveyed in the words of a considerable number of individuals who experienced it firsthand, albeit many years ago, as well as through the recollections of their older friends and family members. Recently, Mr. Kennedy, who witnessed and recorded the narratives, adamantly reiterated the indisputable value of the "Slave Narratives" despite the admitted obstacles. In fact, the unswerving commitment of Mr. Kennedy and his colleagues is strongly attested to by the fact that even after receiving an order from the WPA to stop collecting these narratives, they continued both to seek out former slaves and to record their life stories. When it came time to file these interviews, they simply ascribed code names to them.

The eight chapters in this book mirror the major themes in both the HBO documentary and the documentary material in the Library of Congress Archives. We are fortunate to have enlisted to write the chapter introductions eight scholars who have studied the institution of slavery and the Underground Railroad for many years. They bring their own differ-

ent perspectives to the interpretation of the narratives.

Lonnie G. Bunch, from the Chicago Historical Society, offers insights into the mental as well as physical anguish that accompanies the process of sale. Delores Walters, of Northern Kentucky University, examines the work experience and provides a comparative overview of how labor varied according to geographic regions, type of crops under production, and gender. In his essay on the family, Rex Ellis of the Colonial Williamsburg Foundation gives the reader a sense of the challenges faced by parents as they sought to fortify their children and themselves against the many pains brought on by their condition. Walter Hill, from the National Archives Research Administration, provides a historical perspective on the evolving interpretations of the abuse inherent in slavery developed by scholars in the field. Spencer Crew, of the National Underground Railroad Freedom Center, highlights the battle of wills as slave owners sought to enforce their control over special moments such as weddings and religious services, which the enslaved struggled to keep sacrosanct. One slave response to this tug of war was running away. Keith Griffler, of the University of Cincinnati, illustrates the challenges and repercussions connected with choosing this option. He also points out how strong the desire for freedom was despite the obstacles that lay in the way. Orloff Miller, of the National Underground Railroad Freedom Center, looks at the conditions under which the enslaved existed. He uses archaeological data to examine variations within housing conditions and standards of living. Finally, John Fleming, from the Cincinnati Museum Center, looks at the emancipation story both as an individual experience and as a national struggle. He illustrates how the combined efforts of individuals both enslaved and born free were key to pushing the nation to bring an end to the institution of slavery.

All of the authors recognize the importance of the slave narratives for the human face they place upon the institution of slavery. The narratives remind us of the people affected by this system of enforced labor and the tremendous challenges they faced. But the narratives also contain extraordinary examples of courage and strength of character that are inspiring. These are important lessons for us all to ponder in the context of our lives today. The mission of the National Underground Railroad Freedom Center is to examine the lessons that can be learned from the slave past of the nation and especially the experiences of the participants in the Underground Railroad. The courage, cooperation, and perseverance that emerged from these struggles speak to the impact that people can have both individually and collectively when they decide to work to preserve freedom. The film, the exhibition, and this book, which all emerge from the voices of the slave narratives, parallel the goals of the National Underground Railroad Freedom Center by illustrating the importance of freedom and the reality of the abuses that occur when it is denied.

The kinds of abuses described in the slave narratives have not ended. There are innumerable people in countries worldwide that could relate similar personal experiences. Thus, the slave narratives do more than just document a past era. They offer lessons that resonate for both the past and the present. Our challenge is in how we learn from them and apply them to make a difference in the world we live in today.

—SPENCER CREW, CYNTHIA GOODMAN

. . . Lord, lord child,
what makes you folks wait
so long before you gets this
stuff about way back yonder.
                    --Arthur Greene

Lawdy, honey, yo' caint know
whut a time I had. All cold
n' hungry. No'm, I aint
tellin' no lies. It de gospel
truf. It sho is.
                    --Sarah Gudger

CHAPTER ONE

Slave Auctions

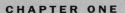

Nothing symbolizes the fragility and inequities of slave life better than the slave auction. Hundreds of thousands of slaves throughout the South experienced the uncertainty, the humiliation, the fear, and the psychological shock that accompanied the domestic slave trade. Yet even for slaves who did not personally experience the slave trade, the slave auction cast a painful shadow over their lives, their hopes for their families, and their belief that "a better day is a-coming."

The end of the International Slave Trade in 1808, coupled with the rapid expansion of plantations into the newly developed regions of Alabama, Mississippi, and Louisiana, led to a renewed demand for slave labor, which was satisfied, in part, by the creation of a system of local and regional slave traders. This domestic slave trade ran the gamut from large businesses located in nearly every major southern city that held regularly scheduled auctions to smaller entities that brought coffles of slaves to the agrarian areas to sell. Usually slave auctions were advertised in local newspaper columns that listed the number and gender of the slaves for sale and often chronicled their particular skills as artisans, strong field hands, or seamstresses, for example. The auction usually allowed for a period of humiliating inspection

and then the slave was led to an elevated stand or auction block. The planters would then shout out their bids and the slave was sold to the highest bidder. The cost for acquiring slaves varied throughout the nineteenth century, depending upon the region and the gender and age of the slave. At the time of the War of 1812, an adult male field hand cost nearly $300, with skilled artisans such as blacksmiths and carpenters costing more. By 1858 in northern Virginia, a prime field hand cost $1,350, with skilled slaves selling for $1,500. Slave women, especially those in the childbearing years, were highly valuable, with some female slaves selling for as much as $1,800 in the years just before the Civil War.

While it is difficult to calculate the number of slaves who went through an auction, the fear and dread of that experience permeated all aspects of slave life and culture. Several of the most venerated spirituals described heaven as a place that had "no more auction blocks for me." And an array of children's songs expressed concern about the stability of the slave family. One song included the line, "Mother, is massa gonna sell us tomorrow?" Why did the specter of the slave auction cast such a long shadow? In many ways, the threat of being sold reflected the capriciousness of a slave's life. The slave's world could change in an instant based on the whims of the owner. Slaves were sold for almost any reason, from the need to settle an estate to an owner's displeasure with a particular slave. In fact, the threat of selling a slave became one of an owner's weapons to enforce discipline and exercise control over the black populace. The fear of being "sold south" was very much a way of life for most slaves. In actuality, so many slaves experienced the auction block that slave life was forced to change throughout the nineteenth century. In the small county of Loudon, Virginia, for example, nearly 7,000 slaves were "sold south."

The domestic slave trade had a devastating impact on African-American life in the eighteenth and nineteenth centuries. Much of the strain fell upon the families, which were easily and often callously disrupted and destroyed when a member was sold. It became very difficult to maintain any semblance of a traditional nuclear family. As the Civil War neared, states in the upper South such as Virginia had a large number of enslaved children who were orphaned by the slave trade. In 1859, nearly 18 percent of the children of slaves had little or no contact with either parent. Marriages also suffered if spouses were separated to meet the economic needs of the slaveowner. Some marriages survived if the couple was only separated by a few miles, commonly known as "marrying abroad." But most couples that were sold rarely saw each other again. The slave trade ensured, according to a Virginia Quaker, that "these people are without their consent torn from their homes, husbands and wives are frequently separated and sold into distant parts, children are taken from their parents without regard to the ties of nature, and the most endearing bonds of affection are broken forever."

Even freedom did not erase the pain and sense of loss that stemmed from the auction block. For many years after the Civil War ended, the newly freed men and women searched throughout the South for the families that were torn from them. Henry Watson recalled how he searched for his mother in the Reconstruction South: "Every exertion was made on my part to find her, or hear some tidings of her. But all my efforts were unsuccessful; and from that day I have never seen or heard from her." So many former slaves were haunted by the sale of loved ones that their search continued for more than a decade. Well into the 1870s and 1880s, African-American newspapers were filled with columns entitled "Information Wanted." These columns contained painful pleas for information about family members who had been separated by slavery. A column from 1870 carries a notice by Charles Gatson, who sought "information of his children, Sam and Betsy Gatson who were sold by a slave trader to go further south to Mississippi or Louisiana. They are now about 22 to 25 years old and were taken away in 1861."

African Americans wrestled with the stigma of the slave auction for many years after the end of slavery. Despite the real losses that the enslaved suffered, African Americans did raise families, maintain marriages, and struggle to find ways to exercise control over their lives in the face of the realization that their bodies were owned by the master.

I remember when they put
'em on the block to sell
'em. The ones 'tween 18
and 30 always bring the
most money. The auctioneer
he stand off at a
distances and cry 'em off
as they stand on the
block. I can hear his
voice as long as I live.
                    --W. L. Bost

W. L. Bost

Lord child, I remember when I was a little boy, 'bout ten years, the speculators come through Newton with droves of slaves. They always stay at our place. The poor critters nearly froze to death. They always come 'long on the last of December so that the niggers would be ready for sale on the first day of January. Many the time I see four or five of them chained together. They never had enough clothes on to keep a cat warm. The women never wore anything but a thin dress and a petticoat and one underwear. I've seen the ice balls hangin' on to the bottom of their dresses as they ran along, jes like sheep in a pasture 'fore they are sheared. They never wore any shoes. Jes run along on the ground, all spewed up with ice. The speculators always rode on horses and drove the pore niggers. When they get cold, they make 'em run 'til they are warm again.

The speculators stayed in the hotel and put the niggers in the quarters jes like droves of hogs. All through the night I could hear them mournin' and prayin'. I didn't know the Lord would let people live who were so cruel. The gates were always locked and they was a guard on the outside to shoot anyone who tried to run away. Lord miss, them slaves look jes like droves of turkeys runnin' along in front of them horses.

I remember when they put 'em on the block to sell 'em. The ones 'tween 18 and 30 always bring the most money. The auctioneer he stand off at a distances and cry 'em off as they stand on the block. I can hear his voice as long as I live.

If the one they going to sell was a young Negro man this is what he say: "Now gentlemen and fellow-citizens here is a big black buck Negro. He's stout as a mule. Good for any kin' o' work an' he never gives any trouble. How much am I offered for him?" And then the sale would commence, and the nigger would be sold to the highest bidder.

If they put up a young nigger woman the auctioneer cry out: "Here's a young nigger wench, how much am I offered for her?" The pore thing stand on the block a shiverin' an' a shakin' nearly froze to death. When they sold, many of the pore mothers beg the speculators to sell 'em with their husbands, but the speculator only take what he want. So maybe the pore thing never see her husban' agin.

W. L. BOST, North Carolina

Dey talks a heap 'bout de niggers stealin'. Well, you know what was de fust stealin' done? Hit was in Afriky, when de white folks stole de niggers jes' like you'd go get a drove o' hosses and sell 'em. Dey'd bring a steamer down dere wid a red flag, 'cause dey knowed dem folks liked red, and when dey see it dey'd follow it till dey got on de steamer. Den when it was all full o' niggers dey'd bring 'em over here and sell 'em.

SHANG HARRIS, Georgia

> 1. SARAH, a mulatress, aged 45 years, a [
> house work in general, is an excellent and faithful nurse for sick persons, and
>
> 2. DENNIS, her son, a mulatto, aged 24 year
> ard for a vessel, having been in that capacity for many years on board one of t
> and a first rate subject.
>
> 3. CHOLE, a mulatress, aged 36 years, she
> the most competent servants in the country, a first rate washer and ironer, do
> wishes a house-keeper she would be invaluable; she is also a good ladies' m
> ity.
>
> 4. FANNY, her daughter, a mulatress, aged
> English, is a superior hair-dresser, (pupil of Guilliac,) a good seamstress a
> rate character.

Talkin' 'bout somethin' awful, you should have been dere. De slave owners was shoutin' and sellin' chillen to one man and de mama and pappy to 'nother. De slaves cries and takes on somethin' awful. If a woman had lots of chillen she was sold for mo', 'cause it a sign she a good breeder.

Right after I was sold to Massa Dunn, dere was a big up-risin' in Tennessee and it was 'bout de Union, but I don't know what it was all about, but dey wanted Massa Dunn to take some kind of a oath, and he wouldn't do it and he had to leave Tennessee. He said dey would take de slaves 'way from him, so he brought me and Sallie Armstrong to Texas. Dere he trades us to Tommy Ellis for some land and dat Massa Ellis, he de best white man that ever lived. He was so good to us we was better off dan when we's free.

MILLIE WILLIAMS, Texas

My mother was separated from her mother when she was three years old. They sold my mother away from my grandmother. She didn't know nothing about her people. She never did see her mother's folks. She heard from them. It must have been after freedom. But she never did get no full understanding about them. Some of them was in Kansas City, Kansas. My grandmother, I don't know what became of her.

When my mother was sold into St. Louis, they would have sold me away from her but she cried and went on so that they bought me too. I don't know nothing about it myself, but my mother told me. I was just nine months old then.

MARY ESTES PETERS, Arkansas

Millie Williams

Negroes Wanted.

THE undersigned wish to purchased a large number of **NEGROES**, of both sexes, for which they will

Pay the Highest Prices in Cash.

Office on Main-street, opposite the Phœnix Hotel, and 2d door above the Statesman Office, Lexington.

SILAS MARSHALL & BRO.

March 15, 1859–50–tf

NEGROES WANTED.

THE undersigned wishes to purchase a large number of sound and healthy

Negroes of both Sexes!

for which the highest price will be paid in cash, at the large residence nearly opposite the Woollen Factory of Thompson & Vandalsem, East Main Street, Lexington, where either himself or his agent, L. C. ROBARDS, may at all times be found.

JOSEPH H. NORTHCUTT.

March 11, '59.   49–tf

Robert Falls was born on December 14, 1840, in the rambling one-story shack that accommodated the fifteen slaves of his Old Marster, Harry Beattie Goforth, on a farm in Claiborne County, North Carolina. His tall frame is slightly stooped, but he is not subjected to the customary infirmities of the aged, other than poor vision and hearing. Fairly comfortable, he is spending his declining years in contentment, for he is now the first consideration of his daughter, Mrs. Lola Reed, with whom he lives. His cushioned rocking chair is the honor seat of the household. His apology for not offering it to visitors, is that he is "not so fast on his feet as he used to be."
—Bella Yoe, WPA Interviewer

Now my father, he was a fighter. He was mean as a bear. He was so bad to fight and so troublesome he was sold four times to my knowing and maybe a heap more times. That's how come my name is Falls, even if some does call me Robert Goforth. Niggers would change to the name of their new marster, every time they was sold. And my father had a lot of names, but kep the one of his marster when he got a good home. That man was Harry Falls. He said he'd been trying to buy father for a long time, because he was the best waggoner in all that country abouts. And the man what sold him to Falls, his name was Collins, he told my father, "You so mean, I got to sell you. You all time complaining about you dont like your white folks. Tell me now who you wants to live with. Just pick your man and I will go see him." Then my father tells Collins, I want you to sell me to Marster Harry Falls. They made the trade. I disremember what the money was, but it was big. Good workers sold for $1,000 and $2,000. After that the white folks didnt have no more trouble with my father. But he'd still fight. That man would fight a she-bear and lick her every time.

ROBERT FALLS, Tennessee

James Green is half American Indian and half Negro. He was born a slave to John Williams, of Petersburg, Va., became a "free boy", then was kidnapped and sold in a Virginia slave market to a Texas ranchman. He now lives at 333 N. Olive St., San Antonio, Texas.
—Unidentified WPA Interviewer

I never knowed my age till after de war, when I's set free de second time, and then marster gits out a big book and it shows I's 25 year old. It shows I's 12 when I is bought and $800 is paid for me. That $800 was stolen money, 'cause I was kidnapped and dis is how it come:

My mammy was owned by John Williams in Petersburg, in Virginia, and I come born to her on dat plantation. Den my father set 'bout to fit me free, 'cause he a full-blooded Indian and done some big favor for a big man high up in de courts, and he gits me set free, and den Marster Williams laughs and call me "free boy."

Then one day along come a Friday and that a unlucky star day and I playin' round de house and Marster Williams come up and say, "Delis, will you 'low Jim walk down the street with me?" My mammy say, "All right, Jim, you be a good boy," and dat de las' time I ever heard her speak, or ever see her. We walks down whar de houses grows close together and pretty soon comes to de slave market. I ain't seed it 'fore, but when Marster Williams says, "Git up on de block," I got a funny feelin', and I knows what has happened. I's sold to Marster John Pinchback and he had de St. Vitus dance and he likes to make he niggers suffer to make up for his squirmin' and twistin' and he the bigges' debbil on earth.

JAMES GREEN, Texas

James Green

Delia Garlic lives at 43 Stone Street, Montgomery, and insists she is 100 years old. Unlike many of the old Negroes of the South, she has no good words for slavery days or the old masters, declaring: "Them days was hell."

She sat on her front porch and assailed the taking of young children from mothers and selling them in different parts of the country.
—Margaret Fowler,
WPA Interviewer

I was growed up when the war come, an' I was a mother befo' it closed. Babies was snatched from dere mother's breas' an' sold to speculators. Chilluns was separated from sisters an' brothers an' never saw each other ag'in.

Course dey cry; you think dey not cry when they was sold lak cattle? I could tell you 'bout it all day, but even den you couldn't guess de awfulness of it.

I never seed none of my brothers an' sisters 'cept brother William. Him an' my mother an' me was brought in a speculator's drove to Richmon' an' put in a warehouse wid a drove of other niggers. Den we was all put on a block an' sol' to de highes' bidder.

DELIA GARLIC, Alabama

I was tol' there was a lot of slave speculators in Chester to buy some slaves for some folks in Alabama. I 'members dat I was took up on a stan' an' a lot of people come 'roun' an' felt my arms an' legs an' chist, an' ast me a lot of questions. Befo' we slaves was took to de tradin' post Ol' Marsa Crawford tol' us to tell eve'ybody what ast us if we'd ever been sick to tell 'em dat us'd never been sick in our life. Us had to tell 'em all sorts of lies for our Marsa or else take a beatin'.

I was jes' a li'l thang; tooked away from my mammy an' pappy, jes' when I needed 'em mos'.

MINGO WHITE, Alabama

Delia Garlic

CHAPTER TWO

Work

Although the British intended otherwise when Jamestown, Virginia, was settled in 1607, Africans replaced white indentured laborers in what became an agricultural colony. Unlike indentured whites, whose freedom was granted after a period of up to five years, black laborers were enslaved for life, thereby racializing Virginia society. By the early eighteenth century, enslaved laborers outnumbered whites. To allay the fears of slave owners, laws forbidding blacks from carrying weapons were passed. On southern plantations in the United States, especially the larger ones required for cotton cultivation, African-American associations provided the basis for establishing a distinct culture and community early in the nineteenth century.

Enslaved persons in the Old South labored mainly in the fields and mainly on cotton plantations; however, cotton epitomized the plantation economy only for a subregion of the South. Groups of the enslaved were essential to tobacco production in Maryland and Virginia, and on South Carolina's rice plantations. Not only were the crops diverse, but the experiences of the laborers within the slavery system were varied as well. Thus, the enslaved worked not only in the fields, but also in the masters' houses as domestics. Rosa Starke's hierarchy of black laborers includes house and groundskeepers (top), skilled craftsmen and foremen (middle), and animal caretakers and field hands (bottom). Overall, nonagri-

cultural work assignments appear arbitrary or inadvertent rather than by design, except for tasks that were defined specifically as women's or men's work. Women worked as healers, midwives, weavers, and seamstresses for both those who were free and those who were not. Similarly, men's responsibilities might extend beyond the fields and the masters' houses as some of them became skilled shipbuilders, crew members, and navigators.

Work in the field was not differentiated on the basis of gender. Accordingly, women such as Sarah Gudger took pride in being able to accomplish even the most arduous farm chores ("I done ebbathin' 'cept split rails"). However, the inadequacies of nineteenth-century obstetrics were compounded by the fact that slave owners believed that black women were more robust than white women and therefore required less treatment during childbirth. Racism as well as sexism meant that black women were viewed differently from either white women or black men by white owners. Under the threat of being sold, enslaved women were pressured to produce as many children as possible in order to reproduce the labor force. As field hands, women were expected to be as productive as men. Yet they were also expected to submit to the sexual demands of the master or his male heirs and hired workers. A woman resisted or complied with these solicitations in many cases depending upon her assessment of the benefits to herself and to present (and future) offspring in doing so. Despite withstanding a system that limited stable marriages among enslaved couples, mothers were often able to instill in their children self-reliance and autonomy.

The slavery system on southern plantations linked the enslaved and their owners to a lifetime of interdependence. Children born into slavery began their initiation into the work routine as exploitable property almost from the cradle. At the other end of the life cycle, women who were beyond childbearing (and too old to work in the field) typically were expected to care for the master's children.

Depending on the crop, enslaved laborers worked more or less in organized "gangs." Because the cultivation of rice was both complex and labor-intensive, more enslaved laborers were required per unit than for either cotton or tobacco cultivation. Therefore, unlike the rice growers, who were organized according to a task system, cotton, tobacco, and sugar growers were organized in work groups that planted, irrigated, harvested, and processed the commodity together. Work gangs were more subject to the direct control of masters and overseers than those whose labor was assigned by task.

There is general agreement by both those who survived slavery and those who study it regarding the inhumane and often brutal work conditions. Domestic service did not mean that the enslaved were subject to less suffering than field hands. Most accounts focus on the physical brutality of the system, including the devices used for whipping and restraining transgressors. However, the mental cruelty endured by enslaved individuals, though harder to document and quantify, must not be underestimated. Stories of mothers desperate to flee the system but forced to recognize the futility of escape convey a sense of the personal anguish they experienced. In coping with the relentless work routines, enslaved persons used both collective forms of resistance such as work slowdowns and individual strategies such as feigning illness. They composed songs with satirical and biting lyrics to comment on their existence and to manage dire working conditions.

Scholars now characterize the slavery system as one of cruel domination, but also one in which enslaved persons experienced considerable diversity. Clear also is that the plantation economy laid the basis for industrial development. The cultural impacts of this oppressive system will be better understood when such works as the building of the nation's capitol are duly recognized and celebrated as the contributions of enslaved laborers.

I recollects once when
I was tryin' to clean
de house like ole
miss tell me, I finds
a biscuit and I's so
hungry I et it, 'cause
we nev'r see sich
a thing as a biscuit
only some times on
Sunday mornin'.
                --Jenny Proctor

Jenny Proctor

Jenny Proctor was born in Alabama in 1850. She was a slave of the Proctor family and began her duties about the house when a very young girl. As soon as she was considered old enough to do field labor she was driven with the other slaves from early morning until late at night. The driver was cruel and administered severe beatings at the slightest provocation. Jenny remained with her owners after the close of the Civil War, not from choice but because they had been kept in such dense ignorance they had no knowledge of how to make their own living. After the death of her master several years later, she and her husband, John Proctor, came to Texas in a mule drawn covered wagon and settled in Leon County near the old town of Buffalo. There they worked as share croppers until the death of her husband. She then came to San Angelo, Texas with her son, with whom she has made her home for many years.

—Unidentified WPA Interviewer

I's hear tell of dem good slave days but I ain't nev'r seen no good times den.

My mother's name was Lisa and when I was a very small chile I hear dat driver goin' from cabin to cabin as early as 3 o'clock in de mornin' and when he comes to our cabin he say, "Lisa, Lisa, git up from dere and git dat breakfast." My mother, she was cook and I don't recollect nothin' 'bout my father. If I had any brothers and sisters I didn't know it.

I 'tended to de chillun when I was a little gal and tried to clean de house jes' like ole miss tells me to.

I recollects once when I was tryin' to clean de house like ole miss tell me, I finds a biscuit and I's so hungry I et it, 'cause we nev'r see sich a thing as a biscuit only some times on Sunday mornin'. We jes' have co'n braid and syrup and some times fat bacon, but when I et dat biscuit and she comes in and say, "Whar dat biscuit?"

I say, "Miss, I et it 'cause I's so hungry." Den she grab dat broom and start to beatin' me over de head wid it and callin' me low down nigger and I guess I jes' clean lost my head 'cause I know'd better den to fight her if I knowed anything 'tall, but I start to fight her and de driver, he comes in and he grabs me and starts beatin' me wid dat cat-o'-nine-tails, and he beats me 'til I fall to de floor nearly dead. He cut my back all to pieces, den dey rubs salt in de cuts for mo' punishment. Lawd, Lawd, honey! Dem was awful days.

JENNY PROCTOR, Texas

My Marster and all de other big white fokes, dey raised pea fouls. Is yu ebber seed any? Well, ev'y spring us little niggers, we coch dem wild things at night. Dey could fly like a buzzard. Dey roosted up in de pine trees, right up in de tip top. So de Missus, she hab us young uns clam up dar and git 'em when dey first took roost.

In dem days de dining room wuz big and had de windows open all de summer long, and all de doos stayed streched too. Quick as de mess of victuals began to come on de table, a little nigger boy was put up in de swing, I calls it, over de table to fan de flies and gnats off'en de Missus' victuals. Dis swing wuz just off'n de end of de long table. Some of de white fokes had steps a leadin' up to it. Some of 'em jus had de little boys maws to fech de young'uns up dar til dey got fru; den dey wuz fetched down again.

Well, when I got my pants, my maw fetched me in and I clumb up de steps dat Marse Johnson had, to git up in his swing wid. At fus, dey had to show me jus how to hole de brush, kaise dem peacock feathers wuz so long, iffen you didn't mind your bizness, de ends of dem feathers would splash in de gravy er sumpin nother, and den de Missus table be all spattered up.

It twad'nt long for I got used to it and I nebber did splash de feathers in no rations. But affen I got used to it, I took to agoin to sleep up thar.

HENRY COLEMAN, South Carolina

Francis Black

Francis Black was born at Grand Bluff, Mississippi, about 1850, on the Jim Carlton plantation. When five years old, she was stolen and taken to the slave market in New Orleans. Failing to sell her there, the slave traders took her to Jefferson, Texas, and sold her to Bill Tumlin. Francis stayed with him five years after she was freed, then married and moved to Cass County, Texas. She became blind a year ago, and now lives at the Ragland Old Folks Home, 318 Elm St., Texarkana, Texas. —Unidentified WPA Interviewer

I played with them two chillen all day, then sot the table, I was so small I'd git in a chair to reach the dishes out of the safe. I had to pull a long flybrush over the table whilst the white folks et.

Marse Tumlin had a farm 'bout four mile from town, and a overseer, and I seed him buckle the niggers crost a log and whip them. Marse lived in Jefferson, heself, and when he'd go to the farm he allus took his boy with him. We'd be playin' in the barn and Marse call from the house, "Come on, Jimmie, we're gwine to the farm." Jimmie allus say to me, "Come on, nigger, let's ride round the farm." I'd say, "I ain't no nigger." He'd say, "Yes, you is, my pa paid $200 for you. He bought you for to play with me."

FRANCIS BLACK, Texas

My job was taking care of the white children up at the Big House (that is what they called the house where our masters lived), and I also had to feed the little Negro children. I remember quite well how those poor little children used to have to eat. They were fed in boxes and troughs, under the house. They were fed corn meal mush and beans. When this was poured into their box they would gather around it the same as we see pigs, horses and cattle gather around troughs today.

OCTAVIA GEORGE, Oklahoma

Martin Jackson, who calls himself a "black Texan", well deserves to select a title of more distinction, for it is quite possible that he is the only living former slave who served in both the Civil War and the World War. He was born in bondage in Victoria Co., Texas, in 1847, the property of Alvy Fitzpatrick. This self-respecting Negro is totally blind, and when a person touches him on the arm to guide him he becomes bewildered and asks his helper to give verbal directions, up, down, right or left. It may be he has been on his own so long that he cannot, at this late date, readjust himself to the touch of a helping hand. His mind is uncommonly clear and he speaks with no Negro colloquialisms and almost no dialect.

Following directions as to where to find Martin Jackson, "the most remarkable Negro in San Antonio," a researcher made his way to an old frame house at 419 Center St., walked up the steps and through the house to an open door of a rear room. There, on an iron bed, lay a long, thin Negro smoking a cigarette. He was dressed in a woolen under-shirt and black trousers and his beard and mustache were trimmed much after the fashion of white gallants of the Gay Nineties. His head was remarkably well-shaped, with striking eminences in his forehead over his brows.

After a moment the intruder spoke and announced his mission. The old Negro, who is stone blind, quickly admitted that he was Martin Jackson, but before making any further comment he carried on an efficient interview himself; he wanted to know who the caller was, who had directed the visit, and just what branch of the Federal service happened to be interested in the days of slavery. These questions satisfactorily answered, he went into his adventures and experiences, embellishing the highlights with uncommon discernment and very little prodding by the researcher.
—Unidentified WPA Interviewer

My earliest recollection is the day my old boss presented me to his son, Joe, as his property. I was about five years old and my new master was only two.

I used to handle a big dictionary three times a day, but it was only to put it on a chair so my young master could sit up higher at the table. I never went to school. I learned to talk pretty good by associating with my masters in their big house.

MARTIN JACKSON, Texas

Dere was just two classes to de white folks, buckra slave owners and poor
white folks dat didn't own no slaves. Dere was more classes 'mongst
de slaves. De fust class was de house servants. Dese was de butler,
de maids, de nurses, chambermaids, and de cooks. De nex' class was
de carriage drivers and de gardeners, de carpenters, de barber, and de
stable men. Then come de nex' class de wheelwright, wagoners, black-
smiths and slave foremen. De nex' class I members was de cow men
and de niggers dat have care of de dogs. All dese have good houses and
never have to work hard or git a beatin'. Then come de cradlers of
de wheat, de threshers, and de millers of de corn and de wheat, and de
feeders of de cotton gin. De lowest class was de common field niggers.

ROSA STARKE, South Carolina

She uster make my aunt Caroline knit all day an' when she git so tired aftah
dark that she'd git sleepy, she'd make 'er stan' up an knit. She work her
so hard that she'd go to sleep standin' up an' every time her haid nod
an' her knees sag, the lady'd come down across her haid with a switch.

ELIZABETH SPARKS, Virginia

Mary Reynolds claims to be more than a hundred years old. She was born in slavery to the Kilpatrick family, in Black River, Louisiana. Mary now lives at the Dallas County Convalescent Home. She has been blind for five years and is very feeble.
—Unidentified WPA Interviewer

The conch shell blowed afore daylight and all hands better git out for roll call or Solomon bust the door down and git them out. It was work hard, git beatin's and half fed. They brung the victuals and water to the fields on a slide pulled by a old mule. Plenty times they was only a half barrel water and it stale and hot, for all us niggers on the hottes' days. Mostly we ate pickled pork and corn bread and peas and beans and 'taters. They never was as much as we needed.

The times I hated most was pickin' cotton when the frost was on the bolls. My hands git sore and crack open and bleed. We'd have a li'l fire in the fields and iffen the ones with tender hands couldn't stand it no longer, we'd run and warm our hands a li'l bit.

[Massa Kilpatrick] raised corn and cotton and cane and 'taters and goobers, 'sides the peas and other feedin' for the niggers. I 'member I helt a hoe handle mighty onsteady when they put a old woman to larn me and some other chillun to scrape the fields. . . . She say, "For the love of Gawd, you better larn it right, or Solomon will beat the breath out you body." Old man Solomon was the nigger driver.

MARY REYNOLDS, Texas

Bells and horns! Bells for dis and horns for dat! All we knowed was go and come by de bells and horns!

Old ram horn blow to send us all to de field. We all line up, about seventy-five field niggers, and go by de tool shed and git our hoes, or maybe go hitch up de mules to de plows.

CHARLEY WILLIAMS, Oklahoma

Charley Williams

I sho' has had a ha'd life. Jes wok, an' wok, an' wok. I nebbah know nothin' but work.

No'm, I nebbah knowed whut it wah t' rest. I jes wok all de time f'om mawnin' till late at night. I had t' do ebbathin' dey wah t' do on de outside. Wok in de field, chop wood, hoe cawn, till sometime I feels lak mah back sholy break.

Ole Boss he send us niggahs out in any kine ob weathah, rain o' snow, it nebbah mattah. We had t' go t' de mountings, cut wood an' drag it down t' de house. Many de time we come in wif ouh cloes stuck t' ouh poah ole cold bodies, but 'twarn't no use t' try t' git 'em dry. Ef de Ole Boss o' de Ole Missie see us dey yell: "Git on out ob heah yo' black thin', an' git yo' wok outen de way!"

Lawdy, honey, yo' caint know whut a time I had. All cold n' hungry. No'm, I aint tellin' no lies. It de gospel truf. It sho is.

SARAH GUDGER, North Carolina

Sarah Gudger

CHAPTER THREE

Family

Nearly three million enslaved Africans worked on farms and in plantations across the South; half that number worked on cotton plantations and the rest cultivated tobacco, rice, and sugar cane. The cotton farm was the typical location for most African Americans during the days of slavery.

Most of these workers were divided into two main categories: field hands and house servants. House servants cared for the house and the gardens, cooked the meals, slaughtered the meat, drove the carriages, and were personal servants to the master and mistress of the household. Field slaves worked hard, long, and often. The cultivation of crops—whether used domestically or for profit—was difficult, backbreaking, and thankless. No discrimination was seen in the fields; men, women, and children (unless they were too old and infirm, or too young) were expected to work.

Such was the reality on which enslaved Africans and African Americans forged a familial structure. The work they performed represented a common condition as well as a shared adversary. It united them in their misery, their shared drudgery, their collective frustration, and their will to survive. The thought of being delivered from their common enemy one day bolstered their determination to forge on. Whether they were blood relatives or not, their collective will to see a better day made them family. They prayed together when their spirits were low, they cried together when one of their number died, and they devised untold schemes to escape the overseer's lash when they could not bear the stifling summer heat another minute.

Because the realities of the plantation system left them socially and culturally isolated, they had to express themselves within its strictures. Only a trusted few were allowed outside the immediate area. Therefore, each day they were reminded of the nature of their existence and the completeness of their alienation from the outside world—a hard truth for any adult, but even more traumatic for a child.

How do an enslaved man and woman fortunate enough to have children—if only for a short while—provide them with an understanding of the life they must lead under the yoke of slavery? How do they explain to a mind born free that their bodies must belong forever to someone else? How does a father let go and resign himself to the fact that the future he wishes for his daughter may give way to his standing by and watching her being raped by a cruel master? How does a mother tell her son that he might not see her in the morning? How does she prepare him for the day when both of them may face the auction block? Josiah Henson lamented just such a case:

> "My brothers and sisters were bid off first, and one by one, while my mother, paralyzed by grief, held me by the hand. Her turn came, and she was bought by Isaac Riley of Montgomery county. Then I was offered to the assembled purchasers. My

mother, half distracted with the thought of parting forever from all her children, pushed through the crowd, while the bidding for me was going on, to the spot where Riley was standing. She fell at his feet, and clung to his knees, entreating him in tones that a mother only could command, to buy her *baby* as well as herself, and spare to her one, at least, of her little ones. Will it, can it be believed that this man, thus appealed to, was capable not merely of turning a deaf ear to her supplication, but of disengaging himself from her with such violent blows and kicks, as to reduce her to the necessity of creeping out of his reach, and mingling the groan of bodily suffering with the sob of a breaking heart? . . . I seem to see and hear my poor weeping mother now."

The shackles of slavery made time precious to the African family, because they never knew how long they would be with their loved ones. The whole concept of extended family and nuclear family was a result of the loss of blood relations resulting from slavery and its emasculation of the nuclear family.

As a larger free black population emerged in the nineteenth century, it had begun to use the boundaries of its servitude to its advantage. As the people learned more and more about the variety of ways they could manipulate their surroundings, they cultivated complex relationships with former masters, merchants, and those who could sponsor, support, or nurture their

efforts toward self-determination. Even at that, they paid a high price for the goods and services they obtained from the white community.

Much of the family life they forged and the relationships they built with one another took place behind closed doors and away from the searching, searing, and suspicious eyes of their captors. Africans and African Americans joined together to drink, gamble, play, frolic, fight, cry, laugh, love, and pray. They did it as often as they could and they did it with abandon, knowing that it too would soon end.

These stories inspire as they tell of the promise of dreams that refused to be deferred, hope trampled but defying defeat, love shackled but not shaken, and eyes wide open to the possibilities of a better day.

I recollect Mammy said
to old Julie, "Take keer
my baby chile (dat was
me) and iffen I never
sees her no mo' raise
her for God." Den she
fell off de waggin where
us was all settin' and
roll over on de groun's
jes' acryin'.
                    --Laura Clark

Laura Clark

Laura Clark, black and wrinkled with her eighty-six years, moved limpingly about the tiny porch of her cabin on the outskirts of Livingston. Battered cans and rickety boxes were filled with a profusion of flowers of the common variety. Laura offered me a split-bottomed chair and lowered herself slowly into a rocker that creaked even under her frail body. "Po'ly, Miss, po'ly," she responded to my query about her health. "Tain't lack de old days. I's crippled and mos' blin' now atter all de years what I got."

—Ruby Pickens Tartt, WPA Interviewer

I was born on Mr. Pleasant Powell's place in North Ca'lina, and when I was 'bout six or seven years old I reckon hit 'twas, Mr. Garret from right up yonder in de bend bout eight miles from Livingston goin' north on de Livingston and Epes Road, bought 10 of us chillun in North Ca'lina and sent two white men and one was Mr. Skinner to fotch us back in waggins. And he fotch ole Julie Powell and Henry to look after us. Wa'n't none of them 10 chillun no kin to me, and he never bought my mammy, so I had to leave her behind.

I recollect Mammy said to old Julie, "Take keer my baby chile (dat was me) and iffen I never sees her no mo' raise her for God." Den she fell off de waggin where us was all settin' and roll over on de groun's jes' acryin'. But us was eatin' candy what dey done give us for to keep us quiet, and I didn't have sense 'nuff for to know what ailed Mammy, but I knows now and I never seed her no mo' in dis life. When I heared from her atter S'render she done dead and buried. Her name was Rachel Powell.

LAURA CLARK, Alabama

My paw's name was Tom Vaughn and he was from the north, born free man and lived and died free to the end of his days. He wasn't no eddicated man, but he was what he calls himself a piano man. He told me once he lived in New York and Chicago and he built the insides of pianos and knew how to make them play in tune. He said some white folks from the south told he if he'd come with them to the south he'd find a lot of work to do with pianos in them parts, and he come off with them.

He saw my maw on the Kilpatrick place and her man was dead. He told Dr. Kilpatrick, my massa, he'd buy my maw and her three chillun with all the money he had, iffen he'd sell her. But Dr. Kilpatrick was never one to sell any but the old niggers who was part workin' in the fields and past their breedin' times. So my paw marries my maw and works the fields, same as any other nigger.

Once massa goes to Baton Rouge and brung back a yaller gal dressed in fine style. He builds her a house 'way from the quarters and she done fine sewin' for the whites. Us niggers knowed the doctor took a black woman quick as he did a white and took any on his place he wanted, and he took them often. But mostly the chillun born on the place looked like niggers.

Onct two of them goes down the hill to the doll house where the Kilpatrick chillun am playin'. They wants to go in the dollhouse and one the Kilpatrick boys say, "That's for white chillun." They say, "We ain't no niggers, 'cause we got the same daddy you has, and he comes to see us near every day and fotches us clothes and things from town." They is fussin' and Missy Kilpatrick is listenin' out her chamber window. She heard them white niggers say, "He is our daddy and we call him daddy when he comes to our house to see our mama."

MARY REYNOLDS, Texas

I'se Marshal Butler, 88 years old and was born on December 25. I knows it
was Christmas Day for I was a gift to my folks. Anyhow, I'se the only
niggah that knows exactly how old he be. I disremembers the year but
you white folks can figure et out.

My Mammy was Harriet Butler and my pappy was John Butler and
we all was raised in Washington-Wilkes.

Mammy was a Frank Collar niggah and her man was of the tribe
of Ben Butler, some miles down de road. Et was one of dem trial
marriages—they'se tried so hard to see each other but old Ben Butler
says two passes a week war enuff to see my mammy on de Collar
plantation. When de war was completed pappy come home to us.

MARSHAL BUTLER, Georgia

Dere am one thing Massa Hawkins does to me what I can't shunt from my
mind. I know he don't do it for meanness, but I allus holds it 'gainst
him. What he done am force me to live with dat nigger, Rufus, 'gainst
my wants.

After I been at he place 'bout a year, de massa come to me and say,
"You gwine live with Rufus in dat cabin over yonder. Go fix it for livin'."
I's 'bout sixteen year old and has no larnin', and I's jus' igno'mus chile.

"Woman, I's pay big money for you and I's done dat for de cause I
wants yous to raise me chillens. I's put yous to live with Rufus for dat
purpose. Now, if you doesn't want whippin' at de stake, yous do what
I wants."

What am I's to do? So I 'cides to do as the massa wish and so I
yields.

ROSE WILLIAMS, Texas

Marshal Butler

Sarah Frances Shaw Graves (Aunt Sally) whose address is R.F.D. #4 Skidmore, Missouri is eighty-seven years of age. She lives with her bachelor son on their one-hundred-twenty acre farm. The home though small is moderately furnished and she enjoys the comforts of the rural telephone and radio and daily newspapers in her home. The house is surrounded by a nice yard containing many flowers and is enclosed with an iron fence, a cement walk leading from the gate to the house.

Aunt Sally had been informed that the reporter was intending to call on her the following day and she was eagerly awaiting the arrival of the visitor. The reporter was greatly impressed by the arrangement and cleanliness of Aunt Sally's modest home. Aunt Sally was immaculately dressed in a stiffly starched print dress and a fresh white apron. Her white hair was combed straight back off her forehead and held back with side combs. She was in a very excited talkative mood, and talked freely, and laughed heartily when the reporter explained the purpose of the interview and asked the privilege of taking her picture.
—Unidentified WPA Interviewer

My name is Sarah Frances Shaw Graves or Aunt Sally as everybody calls me. I am eighty-seven (87) years old and I was born March 23, 1850 in Kentucky somewhere near Louisville. I was brought to Missouri when I was six months old with my Mamma who was a slave owned by a man named Shaw who had alotted her to a man named Jimmie Graves.

We left my Papa in Kentucky as he belonged to another man. My Papa never knew where my Mamma and me went and my Mamma and me never knew where my Papa went.

SARAH FRANCES SHAW GRAVES, Missouri

Sarah Frances Shaw Graves

Living Conditions

Living conditions among the enslaved in antebellum America were nearly as varied as those of the free white population. Slavery was defined not solely by physical circumstance, but also by legal and social status. On larger plantations, social status was reinforced by the layout of the property, with carefully planned distinctions between formal and working spaces. But despite the systematic ordering of law, custom, landscape, and material culture to reinforce social rank, even people in bondage found opportunities for self-expression as a form of resistance. Food, ceramics, agricultural practices, architecture, and even home-lot landscaping presented opportunities for preserving a unique African or African-American identity within the context of slavery. Some of the most intriguing and compelling work on African survivals in the material culture of the African-American enslaved is now emerging from the fields of archaeology and architectural history.

Archaeological investigations conducted at enslavement sites over the past thirty years indicate that the objects of everyday life (the "material culture") of slavery were often a generation or so out of fashion when compared to mainstream white culture. There is also a strong resemblance between the material culture of the enslaved and the sites of an earlier free white frontier in different regions. Slave cabins recapitulate frontier architecture. For example, in the testimonies presented below, when Carter Jackson speaks of the dirt-floored cabin of his Texas childhood, he could have been describing a frontier cabin of an earlier generation.

The same observation plays out for dietary studies ("foodways") and the ceramics in which food was stored and served. The less-than-ideal foods typical of a frontier or an earlier generation are also typical in the slave quarters. In fact, the archaeological remains of food found at the sites of poor whites of the same generation are often indistinguishable from those of the enslaved. Ceramic designs that might have been fashionable in the previous generation dominate assemblages of the enslaved, indicating a hand-me-down introduction to mass-produced goods.

However, the frontiersmen and poor whites had one thing the enslaved did not; their freedom. The lives of the enslaved depended almost entirely upon the whim of the enslaver. Again and again, the narratives of freed slaves equate their living conditions to the character of their masters. Subtleties of dress and privilege we of the twenty-first century might miss are remembered with pride or anger. In the narratives below, that perception of want or sufficiency is described in a variety of ways. Jack Maddox's account of slave children begging for scraps at the kitchen door or memories of abiding childhood hunger dramatize an endemic, offhand brutality. Yet Jack's wife, Rosa, paints

a very different picture, of antebellum housewives sharing their garden produce with the household slaves.

Even in the most horrific circumstances, human beings take comfort where they can and

In the modern revulsion to slavery as an institution, the idea of being treated as property would seem to transcend even the most comfortable physical circumstances. Yet Rosa Maddox believed that "all we freed for is to starve to death," remembering her grim years as a Reconstruction refugee. Perhaps idealism is itself a luxury.

In reading these narratives, it is important to remember that we do not know to what extent the informants were "playing up" to the interviewers, telling what they thought their recorder wanted to hear. But even if both the good and the bad times were amplified by time and bias, most memories of any kind of comfort or happiness seem to center around opportunities for community formation. In all cases, fleeting moments of happiness seem to have been held together by community ties vulnerable to the next slave auction.

At the time our informants were interviewed, they were remembering yearnings dating from enslavement, yearnings that had been more or less fulfilled for over sixty years. The narratives are at their most powerful when describing the bedrock knowledge of daily, systematic, immutable exploitation. Jack Maddox said that if white folks got to heaven they would turn it wrong side out, "and have the angels working to make something they could take away from them." That worldview burns in the belly down through the generations.

remember it as happiness. Lucindy Lawrence Jurdon remembered ritualized flirting and corn-shucking parties with dancing and music. Other accounts recall the central role of churches or less formal religious observances.

I tell you de truth,
slave time wuz slave
time wid us. My brother
wore his shoes out,
and had none all thu
winter. His feet
cracked open and bled
so bad you could track
him by the blood.
                    --Louisa Adams

Louisa Adams

Marster worked us hard and gave us nuthin. We had to use what we made in the garden to eat. We also et our hogs. Our clothes were bad, and beds were sorry. We went barefooted in a way. What I mean by that is, that we had shoes part of the time. We got one pair o' shoes a year. When dey wored out we went barefooted. Sometimes we tied them up with strings, and they were so ragged de tracks looked like bird tracks, where we walked in the road. We lived in log houses, daubed with mud. They called 'em the slaves houses. My old daddy partly raised his chillluns on game. He caught rabbits, coons, an' possums. He would work all day and hunt at night. We had no holidays. They did not give us any fun as I know. I could eat anything I could git. I tell you de truth, slave time wuz slave time wid us. My brother wore his shoes out, and had none all thu winter. His feet cracked open and bled so bad you could track him by the blood.

LOUISA ADAMS, North Carolina

Charley Mitchell, farmer in Panola Co., Texas, was born in 1852, a slave of Nat Terry, an itinerant Baptist preacher of Lynchburg, Virginia. Charley left the Terrys one year after he was freed. He worked in a tobacco factory, then as a waiter, until 1887, when he moved to Panola Co. For fifty years he has farmed in the Sabine River bottom, about twenty-five miles southeast of Marshall, Texas.
—Unidentified WPA Interviewer

Course, I didn't git no schoolin'. The white folks allus said niggers don't need no larnin'. Some niggers larnt to write their initials on the barn door with charcoal, then they try to find out who done that, the white folks, I mean, and say they cut his fingers off iffen they jus' find out who done it.

CHARLEY MITCHELL, Texas

None of us was 'lowed to see a book or try to learn. Dey say we git smarter den dey was if we learn anything, but we slips around and gits hold of dat Webster's old blue back speller and we hides it 'til way in de night and den we lights a little pine torch and studies dat spellin' book. We learn it too.

JENNY PROCTOR, Texas

Jack and Rosa Maddox, married couple, both ex-slaves. Jack Maddox, born about 1849 in slavery to the Maddox family in Marion County, Georgia, near Buena Vista. Rosa Maddox, born about 1848 in slavery to the Andrews family in Mississippi. Rosa and Jack Maddox were married in December 1869 in Union Parish, Louisiana; now live at 2713 Gaston Avenue, Dallas, Texas. They subsist on the old age pension.
—Unidentified WPA Interviewer

JACK: Yes I was born a slave and so was Rosa. We got out of the chattel slavery and I was better off for gettin' out but Rosa don't think so. She says all we freed for is to starve to death. I guess she's right 'bout that, too, for herself. She says her whitefolks were good to her. But don't you expect me to love my whitefolks. I love them like a dog loves hickory.

I was settin' here thinking the other night 'bout the talk of them kind of whitefolks going to Heaven. Lord God, they'd turn the Heaven wrong side out and have the angels working to make something they could take away from them. I can say these things now. I'd say them anywhere—in the courthouse—before the judges, before God. 'Cause they done done all to me that they can do. I'm done past everything but worryin' 'bout Rosa 'cause she don't get 'nuf to eat and 'cause she feel bad all the time. But they ain't no complainin' in her—(to Rosa), Mama, how you feel in the sun?

ROSA: Best to be expected this time o' year.

JACK: I was born in Georgia on a farm. My mother's name was Lucindy. I heard other Negroes say she was a good woman but she died when I was a little boy, not more than three or four. She left my little brother a crawlin' baby 'bout eleven months old. I can remember a little her dyin'. I can remember her rockin' me on the steps and singin', "Lord revive us. All our help must come from Thee." I can remember cryin' for my mama and bein' lonesome for her. They tried to tell me she was dead but I couldn't get it through my little head. My little brother was pitiful—plumb pitiful. There was one between me and the baby and all of us lonesome for our mama. I had a older brother and a older sister. My sister was so good. She wasn't nothing but a chap but she did what she could for us.

Many times when she wasn't but nine years old I have held a pine torch for her to see how to wash our rags at night. Then Judge Maddox's cook was a good woman. She was half sister to Judge Maddox and was a sister-in-law to my mama. For a long time she let the baby sleep with her in her bed.

But my other brothers and sisters had to sleep on the floor in the cabin huddled together in cold weather so we wouldn't freeze to death. Our life was a misery. I hate the white man every time I think of being no more than animals.

Judge Maddox moved into Buena Vista when I was real small. He had a big fine double run frame house covering a large piece of ground. We used to wait outside the kitchen door of the master's big house. The baby would crawl up by the door and wait with us. The cook would give us what she could. Sometimes she would give us a teaspoon of syrup and we would mix it with water to make something sweet. I used to crave sweet. Or we would eat a biscuit with fried meat grease on it. We used to be too hungry to give the baby his rightful share. We would get the chicken feet where they threw them out and roast them in the ashes and gnaw the bone.

Judge Maddox had about fifty slaves as I remember when I was a little boy. Most of them stayed out on the farm and worked out there.

My father was a blacksmith. He could make everything from a horseshoe nail to a gooseneck. He was sold to Judge Maddox from the Burkhalters. My father said the Burkhalters were mean as they come. He said that his master, Mr. Burkhalter, had gone to a war when he was a young man and stayed six months. He told me that there had always been wars and there would always be wars and rumors of wars as long as the world stands.

Rosa never did know nothin' 'bout her father, eh mama?

ROSA: That's right, I never did know nothing 'bout my paw but I looked on my mama like a savior. Her name was Hannah Clemon and Dr. Andrews my master had always owned her. Dr. Andrews was a good man and a good liver. He was from Mississippi but he moved to Union Parish, Louisiana, when I was such a little girl I don't remember.

My mama said that she remembered when Dr. Andrews came from Louisiana to Mississippi and got married. He brought her along and told her to piece quilts. She said all the time she had to work in the house and piece quilts so much that she didn't have no time a'tall. But he moved back to Louisiana.

Dr. Andrews had 'bout twelve slaves. I had all the time to play until I was 'bout nine years old. We made rag dolls and played dolls. That was me and the other little niggers. I was the baby of my mama. She had eight chillun besides me. We used to play church. We would play singin' and prayin' and dyin'.

Comes to me sometimes little play-game songs. We played something we called "Reglar, reglar, roll over." We sing:

Reglar, reglar
All roll over
Old cow died for want of cold water
Reglar, reglar—
All roll over.

Then 'nuther one was:

Hat, old hat
Looks like a crow's nest
Settin' on a limb

We had good little cabins. There was four of them settin' out in the yard. And we had cotton mattresses and blankets. We had 'nuf to eat too. They 'lowanced it out to us every two weeks. They'ud give us syrup, meal, flour and meat, potatoes and plenty of milk. The madam, that's Miss Fannie, Dr. Andrews' wife, had a garden and she give us fresh greens and onions and things.

The neighbors used to say, "There goes Oat Andrews' free niggers." Thats cause he never hardly whipped them and give them rest and play time. He doctored us when we was sick and took good care of us. I sho' thought a heap o' Dr. Andrews.

JACK and ROSA MADDOX, Texas

Back in Alabama, Missie Adeline Carter took me when I was past my creepin'
days to live in the big house with the white folks. I had a room built
on the big house, where I stayed, and they was allus good to me, 'cause
I's one of their blood. They never hit me a lick or slapped me once, and
told me they'd never sell me away from them.

I had one brother and one sister I helped raise. They was mostly
nigger. The Carters told me never to worry 'bout them, though, 'cause
my mammy was of their blood and all of us in our fam'ly would never
be sold, and sometime they'd make free men and women of us. My
brother and sister lived with the niggers, though.

My massa used to give me a li'l money 'long, to buy what I wanted.
I allus bought fine clothes. In the summer when I was a li'l one, I wore
lowerin's, like the rest of the niggers. That was things made from
cotton sackin'. Most the boys wore shirttails till they was big yearlin's.
When they bought me red russets from the town, I cried and cried. I
didn't want to wear no rawhide shoes. So they took 'em back. They had
a weakness for my cryin'. I did have plenty fine clothes, good woolen
suits they spinned on the place, and doeskins and fine linens. I druv in
the car'age with the white folks and was 'bout the mos' dudish nigger
in them parts.

CATO CARTER, Texas

Cato Carter

Carter J. Jackson

Parson Rogers come to Texas in '63 and brung 'bout 42 slaves and my first
work was to tote water in the field. Parson lived in a good, big frame
house, and the niggers lived in log houses what had dirt floors and
chimneys, and our bunks had rope slats and grass mattress. I sho'
wish I could have cotch myself sleepin' on a feather bed them days.
I wouldn't woke up till Kingdom Come.

We et vegetables and meat and ash cake. You could knock you
mammy in the head, eatin' that ash cake bread. I ain't been fit since.

CARTER J. JACKSON, Texas

Sometimes massa let niggers have a li'l patch. They'd raise 'taters or goobers.
They liked to have them to help fill out on the victuals. 'Taters roasted
in the ashes was the best tastin' eatin' I ever had. I could die better
satisfied to have jus' one more 'tater roasted in hot ashes. The niggers
had to work the patches at night and dig the 'taters and goobers at
night. Then if they wanted to sell any in town they'd have to git a pass
to go. They had to go at night, 'cause they couldn't ever spare a hand
from the fields.

MARY REYNOLDS, Texas

Lucindy Lawrence Jurdon bustled feverishly about her tiny Lee County cabin when she learned her picture was "goin' to be tuk." She got out her old spinning wheel; sat down before it and beamed.

Her daughter coming in from the field, exclaimed: "Ma, I done tol' you dis lady was comin' to see you; an' you wouldn't believe me." After she had posed, she seated herself to tell about slavery days. Her oldest grandson was sick in the next room with pneumonia; the cabin was stuffy and bare.
—Preston Klein, WPA Interviewer

My mammy was a fine weaver and did de work for both white an' colored. Dis is her spinning wheel, an' it can still be used. I use it sometimes now. Us made our own cloth an' our stockings, too.

I 'members dat when us courted us went to walk an' hunted chestnuts. Us would string dem an' put 'em 'round our necks an' smile at our fellers.

On Sattidy nights dey would have dances an' dance all night long. Somebody would clap hands, beat pans, blow quills or pick de banjer strings. When us had cornshuckin's dey would pile de corn up, ring 'round it an' shuck, drink likker an' holler: "Boss man, boss man, please gimme my time; Boss man, boss man, fer I'm most broke down."

LUCINDY LAWRENCE JURDON, Alabama

Nawsuh, us wan't never given no money for nothin', but I learnt how to make baskets an' I would take 'em in to Talladega on Sat'day evenings an' sell 'em to de white folks for fifteen cents. Den when I needed somp'n lak 'bacca or a little piece of chocolate, I could go to do sto' an' buy it. Lots of slaves on yuther plantations warn't 'lowed to make any money dough.

TOM McALPIN, Alabama

Lucindy Lawrence Jurdon

My mammy she work in de fiel' all day and piece and quilt all night. Den she hab to spin enough thread to make four cuts for de white fo'ks ebber night. Why sometime I nebber go to bed. Hab to hold de light for her to see by. She hab to piece quilts for de white folks too. Why dey is a scar on my arm yet where my brother let de pine drip on me. Rich pine war all de light we ebber hab. My brother was a holdin' de pine so's I can help mammy tack de quilt and he go to sleep and let it drop.

FANNIE MOORE, North Carolina

John W. Fields, 2120 North Twentieth Street, Lafayette, Indiana, now employed as a domestic by Judge Burnett is a typical example of a fine colored gentleman, who, despite his lowly birth and adverse circumstances, has labored and economized until he has acquired a respected place in his home community. He is the owner of three properties, un-mortgaged, and is a member of the colored Baptist Church of Lafayette. As will later be seen his life has been one of constant effort to better himself spiritually and physically. He is a fine example of a man who has lived a morally and physically clean life.

—Cecil C. Miller, WPA Interviewer

In most of us colored folks was the great desire to able to read and write. We took advantage of every opportunity to educate ourselves. The greater part of the plantation owners were very harsh if we were caught trying to learn or write. It was the law that if a white man was caught trying to educate a Negro slave, he was liable to prosecution entailing a fine of fifty dollars and a jail sentence. We were never allowed to go to town and it was not until after I ran away that I knew that they sold anything but slaves, tobacco and wiskey. Our ignorance was the greatest hold the South had on us. We knew we could run away, but what then? An offender guilty of this crime was subjected to very harsh punishment.

JOHN W. FIELDS, Indiana

John W. Fields

CHAPTER FIVE

Abuse

Slavery in the Western Hemisphere was made up of a series of complex relationships. First and foremost, and from the perspective of the enslaved and those who opposed the institution, slavery represented a debasement in human relationships. Power—the will to control one another's life, liberty, and labor—was the basis of the relationship between slave owner and the enslaved. Slave owners had the right to do whatever they deemed necessary to gain profit from their slaves.

Despite the evolution of the institution in the Atlantic black diaspora, one element remained in perpetuity: violence. No matter how we characterize, define, view, examine, analyze, and discuss the institution, violence is its most consistent feature. Embedded in the behavioral notions and concepts of power is the ability to punish and abuse. Slave owners quickly resorted to punishment and abuse to maintain the control of their slave population. Violence often characterizes relationships when control is sought; human nature responds to circumstances when its well-being is threatened. Enslavement must be understood as an extraordinary human crucible, and the enslaved responded in a variety of ways to resist and escape.

In the last thirty years, scholars have restructured how we view and understand slavery. They have raised critical questions about the institution, and the answers have brought us closer to understanding its mechanics and interpersonal relationships. We now have the ability to assess the realities of plantation life and urban bondage because scholars have examined older models of the institution from new and different angles. One emerging view is that slavery was a fractious and fragile institution. We have always perceived slavery as dominance and power over the lives of the enslaved. This perception is correct, but now we also see how resistance and escape played out in the relationship between slave owners and the enslaved. Slave discipline and control formed the basis of this relationship and became a fundamental element in the whole structure of human relationship within the institution.

The Africans brought to the Western Hemisphere did not come willingly, yet slave owners called for and demanded obedience and discipline at any price. Stringent measures were put in place to safeguard it, and individual masters established their own forms of control to force labor out of the enslaved. Owners believed the use of force was appropriate to motivate the enslaved to work, to establish discipline, and to maintain order. Owners enacted severe punishment for dereliction of duties, stealing, challenging orders and authorities, disobedience, indolence, escape, and refusal to submit to their will. Mutilation, branding, whippings, hand and foot stocks, and solitary confinement were characteristic of slavery's violent nature. Rape and the sale of family members resonated viciously throughout the institution.

Violence spared no one. Women and children were just as susceptible as men. In many slave societies, women could be intransigent and on average were punished and abused more than men. Throughout the United States and Caribbean slave societies, plantation managers and overseers reported that women routinely resisted work and were a constant source of frustration. This led to frequent punishment by whipping upon their back and buttock areas, confinement in hand and foot stockades, solitary confinement, and attachment of collars. The extent of the practice led to legislation by the 1820s in many British Caribbean slave societies to prohibit such severe punishment of women. In the American South, despite varied legislation as to the protection of female slaves, the punishment by whipping remained a permanent feature. Owners were careful to protect their vested interest in the institution, and control and discipline at all costs dictated their motives and actions.

Violence intended to intimidate and punish was the method used to instill discipline and maintain control. Cruel and brutal treatment met those who defied the institution. Slaves displayed signs of their defiance with marks of the whip on their backs, irons on their ankles, brands on the face and other parts of their bodies, and missing fingers, ears, eyes, and toes. Intimidation succeeded with some and failed with others. Certainly the severe punishment had an effect both on those who witnessed it and on those who experienced such treatment.

A variety of personalities and reactions came to fruition as the enslaved adjusted and accommodated to a host of experiences. They negotiated and measured how far they could go and crossed boundaries that often led to severe treatment or death. They demonstrated their desire to be freed and to control as much of their lives as possible, and exploited the cracks and crevices in an institution built on power and force but wrought with a fragility that could be swayed in their way. They knew and understood that defiance and escape meant severe risk to their well-being, but they were willing to take the chance. Abuse and punishment upon their body and spirit failed to defeat the desire for freedom.

She say Marse Tom
got mad at the
cookin' and grabs
her by the hair
and drug her out
the house and
grabs the saw off
the tool bench and
whips her.
  --William Moore

William Moore

William Moore was born a slave of the Waller family, in Selma, Alabama, about 1855. His master moved to Mexia, Texas, during the Civil War. William now lives at 1016½ Good Street, Dallas, Texas.
—Unidentified WPA Interviewer

Marse Tom was a fitty man for meanness. He jus' 'bout had to beat somebody every day to satisfy his cravin'. He had a big bullwhip and he stake a nigger on the ground and make 'nother nigger hold his head down with his mouth in the dirt and whip the nigger till the blood run out and red up the ground. We li'l niggers stand round and see it done. Then he tell us, "Run to the kitchen and git some salt from Jane." That my mammy, she was cook. He'd sprinkle salt in the cut, open places and the skin jerk and quiver and the man slobber and puke. Then his shirt stick to his back for a week or more.

My mammy had a terrible bad back once. I seen her tryin' to git the clothes off her back and a woman say, "What's the matter with you back?" It was raw and bloody and she say Marse Tom done beat her with a handsaw with the teeth to her back. She died with the marks on her, the teeth holes goin' crosswise her back. When I's growed I asks her 'bout it and she say Marse Tom got mad at the cookin' and grabs her by the hair and drug her out the house and grabs the saw off the tool bench and whips her.

WILLIAM MOORE, Texas

If nigger went out without a pass de "Paddle-Rollers" would get him. De
    white folks were the "Paddle-Rollers" and had masks on their faces.
    They looked like niggers wid de devil in dere eyes. They used
    no paddles—nothing but straps—wid de belt buckle fastened on.

    Yes sah! I got paddled. Et happened dis way. I'se left home one
Thursday to see a gal on the Palmer plantation—five miles away.
Some gal! No, I didn't get a pass—de boss was so busy! Everything
was fine until my return trip. I wuz two miles out an' three miles to go.
There come de "Paddle-Rollers" I wuz not scared—only I couldn't
move. They give me thirty licks—I ran the rest of the way home. There
was belt buckles all over me. I ate my victuals off de porch railing.
Some gal! Um-m-h. Was worth that paddlin' to see that gal—would do
it over again to see Mary de next night.

> O Jane! love me lak you useter,
> O Jane! chew me lak you useter,
> Ev'y time I figger, my heart gits bigger,
> Sorry, sorry, can't be yo' piper any mo'.

Um-m-mh! Some gal!

MARSHAL BUTLER, Georgia

One day I remembers my brother, January wuz cotched ober seein' a gal on de next plantation. He had a pass but de time on it done gib out. Well suh, when the massa found out dat he wuz a hour late, he got as mad as a hive of bees. So when brother January he come home, de massa took down his long mule skinner and tied him to a rope to a pine tree. He strip' his shirt off and said:

"Now, nigger, I'm goin' to teach you some sense."

Wid dat he started layin' on de lashes. January was a big, fine lookin' nigger, de finest I ever seed. He wuz jus' four years older dan me, an' when de massa begin a beatin' him, January neber said a word. De massa got madder and madder kaze he couldn't make January holla.

"What's de matter wid you, nigger?" he say. "Don't it hurt?"

January, he neber said nothin', and de massa keep a beatin' till little streams of blood started flowin' down January's chest, but he neber holler. His lips wuz a quiverin' and his body wuz a shakin', but his mouf it neber open; and all de while I sat on my mammy's and pappy's steps a cryin'. De niggers wuz all gathered about and some uv 'em couldn't stand it; dey hadda go inside dere cabins. Atter while, January, he couldn't stand it no longer hisself, and he say in a hoarse, loud whisper:

"Massa! Massa! Have mercy on dis poor nigger."

WILLIAM COLBERT, Alabama

William Colbert

Sarah Ashley, 93, was born
in Mississippi. She recalls her
experiences when sold on
the block in New Orleans, and

on a cotton plantation in Texas.
She now lives at Goodrich,
Texas.
—Unidentified WPA Interviewer

I seed a man run away and de white men got de dogs and dey kotch him
and put him in de front room and he jump through de big window and
break de glass all up. Dey sho' whips him when dey kotches him.

De way dey whip de niggers was to strip 'em off naked and whip 'em
till dey make blisters and bus' de blisters. Den dey take de salt and red
pepper and put in de wounds. After dey wash and grease dem and put
somethin' on dem, to keep dem from bleed to death.

SARAH ASHLEY, Texas

My mother's mistress had three boys, one twenty-one, one nineteen, and
one seventeen. Old mistress had gone away to spend the day one day.
Mother always worked in the house. She didn't work on the farm in
Missouri. While she was alone, the boys came in and threw her down
on the floor and tied her down so she couldn't struggle, and one
after the other used her as long as they wanted for the whole afternoon.
Mother was sick when her mistress came home. When old mistress
wanted to know what was the matter with her, she told her what the
boys had done. She whipped them and that's the way I came to be here.

MARY ESTES PETERS, Arkansas

Sarah Ashley

I wuz one slave dat de poor white man had his match. See Miss Sue? Dese here ol' white man said, "what I can't do by fair means I'll do by foul." One tried to throw me, but he couldn't. We tusseled an' knocked over chairs an' when I got a grip I scratched his face all to pieces; an der wuz no more bothering Fannie from him; but oh, honey, some slaves would be beat up so, when dey resisted, an' sometimes if you'll 'belled de overseer would kill yo'. Us Colored women had to go through a plenty, I tell you.

FANNIE BERRY, Virginia

Did de dirty suckers associate wid slave wimmen? I call 'em suckers—feel like saying something else but I'll 'spec [respect] ya, honey. Lord chile, dat wuz common. Marsters an' overseers use to make slaves dat wuz wid deir husbands git up, do as dey say. Send husbands out on de farm, milkin' cows or cuttin' wood. Den he gits in bed wid slave himself. Some women would fight an tussel. Others would be 'umble—feared of dat beatin'. What we saw, couldn't do nothing 'bout it. My blood is bilin' now [at the] thoughts of dem times. Ef dey told dey husbands he wuz powerless.

Are ya tellin' me God ain't er—er—punishing 'em? Lord, Lord, I keep telling ya dem wuz terrible, terrible times. When babies came dey ain't exknowledge 'em. Treat dat baby like 'tothers—nuthing to him. Mother feard to tell 'cause she know'd what she'd git. Dat wuz de concealed part.

I know our overseer we all thought wuz doin' wrong wid dis slave gal but we wuz feard to say hit. When de chile come 'twas white.

One day all de little chillun wuz in yard playing—running 'roun. An de gal's husband wuz settin' near de do' wid de baby in his arms—rockin' away—looking in child's face an' at de chillun playin' in de yard. Wife wuz tendin' to sumpin in de house. All at once he called her an' sed, "Ole lady, dis chile ain't like our other chillun." She say, "Ole man, er—er—stop stedin' [studying] so much foolishness." He dar rockin' de chile looking down at hit and says, "Dis chile is got blue eyes. Dis chile is got white fingernails. Dis chile is got blue eyes jes like our overseer." "Ole man, I don' tole ya, stop settin' dar stedin' so much foolishness! Ole man, you kno' jes as well as I kno', de mornin' I sent ya to Aint Manervia's to git dat buttermilk. Dat wuz six months gone—March an' setch, April an tetaple, May an' dat"—Ha, ha, ha. Dats 3 months she counted. Ha! Ha! Ha! Foolin' de ole man.—He sed, "Yas, dat is nine months." Den he satisfied hit wuz his chile. De pint I'm at is, she wuz feard to tell on overseer den. I don' witness everything I tell ya an' knowd de gal.

REV. ISHRAEL MASSIE, Virginia

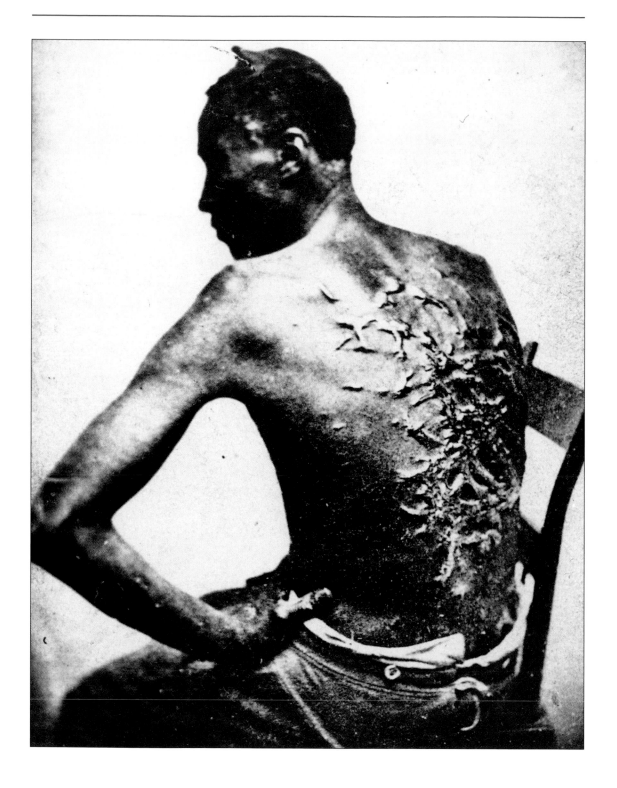

They was a white overseer on the place, and mammy's stepdaddy, Kit, was
    niggerdriver and done all the whippin'. 'Cept of mammy. She was bad
    'bout fightin and the overseer allus tended to her. One day he come to
    the quarters to whip her and she up and throwed a shovel full of live
    coals from the fireplace in his bosom and run out the door. He run her
    all over the place 'fore he cotched her. I seed the overseer tie her down
    and whip her. The niggers wasn't whipped much 'cept for fightin'
    'mongst themselves.

RICHARD JACKSON, Texas

If I had my life to live over I would die fighting rather than be a slave again.
    I want no man's yoke on my shoulders no more.
        They didn't half feed us either. They fed the animals better. They
    gives the mules, ruffage and such, to chaw on all night. But they didn't
    give us nothing to chaw on. Learned us to steal, that's what they done.
    Why we would take anything we could lay our hands on, when we was
    hungry. Then they'd whip us for lieing when we say we dont know
    nothing about it. But it was easier to stand, when the stomach was full.

ROBERT FALLS, Tennessee

CHAPTER SIX

Special Occasions

As a system of forced labor, slavery as it evolved in the United States sought to control the minds and the hearts of its victims. To accomplish this goal they were constantly reminded in obvious and subtle ways of the power slave owners had over every aspect of their lives. The more obvious illustration of this power was the physical punishment meted out to slaves for sundry reasons ranging from working too slow to failing to obey orders to running away. The laws established regarding slavery placed almost absolute power of life and death over the enslaved in the hands of slaveholders. And they did not shy away from exercising that power. Writings about slavery in the United States are replete with vivid descriptions of the physical abuse suffered by enslaved African Americans. The goal was to make them docile and submissive—to deprive them of their humanity. Though these punishments left them scarred, battered, and maimed, they did not necessarily break their spirit or their sense of self-worth. But this struggle was a precarious balancing act.

Even within the oppressive atmosphere of slavery there were ways in which the enslaved found comfort and support within their own community. Moments squeezed from the regimen of most of their days allowed them for a few precious hours to relate to one another in a different manner. In most instances it was the

period in the evening after the day's work was completed, when they were away from the constant, probing gaze of the slaveholder or the overseer, that they could find time for one another. It was then that parents could nurture their children, offering them love and words of wisdom for enduring their condition. It was the time when as a community the enslaved might exchange important information or find ways of escaping the harsh realities of their existence through story telling or the singing of songs or other forms of amusement. The chance to talk and laugh, to support one another, was critical to their survival. It allowed dignity back into their lives and reminded them they were important at least to their families and friends.

It reminded them they did have some control over their own lives and need not give in entirely to those who held them in bondage. Scholars of African-American history and culture such as Sterling Brown, Lawrence Levine, and Sterling Stuckey have noted the importance of these activities in the lives of the enslaved. They were important spiritual wellsprings for enslaved African Americans to return to in moments of self-doubt or depression.

These private moments were particularly significant because more public expressions of joy, grief for the loss of a loved one, or religious convictions were not as readily available to enslaved African Americans. Slaveholders frequently used important occasions to reinforce their control. Weddings, birthdays, Christmas, New Year's, and other normally happy events were subject to the slaveholder's guidelines. Christmas, for example, could be a particularly bittersweet time. In her biography *Incidents in the Life of a Slave Girl*, Linda Brent recalled that while the Christmas holiday usually gave the slaves on her plantation four or five days of celebrating, their revelry was undermined by the knowledge of the painful moments that lay just ahead: the first day of the New Year always brought an auction. Families and loved ones were torn apart and sent to work for strangers, perhaps never to see one another again. Their slaveholder clearly understood the impact of his timing as he decided who was sold, further reinforcing his power.

Church gatherings and funerals were affected by similar efforts to control the enslaved. The extent of the restrictions depended upon the philosophy or even the mood of the slaveholder. More lenient individuals might allow greater freedom than others, but the reality was that the enslaved rarely were given free rein to conduct these activities as they wished. Religious gatherings were a source of contention. African-American forms of Christian worship did not follow the more solemn European pattern. They folded in African rituals that emphasized the oneness with nature and their ancestors. This combination made for highly emotional services that worried slaveholders. Consequently they sought to control these meetings to ensure

that a philosophy of submissiveness was conveyed. Enslaved preachers were expected to advocate this perspective, as were white ministers. Some of the African-American preachers subverted this pressure through the kind of religious doublespeak that historian Charles Joyner describes as the African tradition of "indirection." This device allowed them to criticize the authority and cruelty of slaveholders without confronting them directly. But this approach was problematic and dangerous, especially for the preachers. Secret religious gatherings out of view of slaveholders and other whites gave enslaved African Americans the opportunity to worship in a manner that had more meaning to them, and the spiritual lift they gave the participants was an important survival tool.

Special occasions, which are normally important moments of celebration or reflection, were battlegrounds between slaveholders and the enslaved. In the eyes of the slaveholders the success of the institution revolved around their ability to, as historian Kenneth Stampp noted, "make them stand in fear." For the enslaved it was a battle to preserve their humanity in an inhumane system. The struggle was a mighty one between two determined forces, but what is clear, as we see in the words of formerly enslaved African Americans, is that the human spirit manages to survive even under the severest attack.

After de weddin' we went
down to de cabin Mis'
Betsy done all dressed up,
but Exter couldn' stay no
longer den dat night
kaze he belonged to Marse
Snipes Durham an' he had
to back home.
  --Tempie Herndon Durham

Tempie Herndon Durham

When I growed up I married Exter Durham. He belonged to Marse Snipes
Durham who had de plantation 'cross de county line in Orange County.
We had a big weddin'. We was married on de front po'ch of de big
house. Marse George killed a shoat an' Mis' Betsy had Georgianna, de
cook, to bake a big weddin' cake all iced up white as snow wid a bride
an' groom standin' in de middle holdin' han's. De table was set out in
de yard under de trees, an' you ain't never seed de like of eats. All de
niggers come to de feas' an' Marse George had a dram for everybody.
Dat was some weddin'. I had on a white dress, white shoes an' long
white gloves dat come to my elbow, an' Mis' Betsy done made me a
weddin' veil out of a white net window curtain.

After Uncle Edmond said de las' words over me an' Exter, Marse
George got to have his little fun: He say, "Come on, Exter, you an'
Tempie got to jump over de broom stick backwards; you got to do dat
to see which one gwine be boss of your househol'." Everybody come
stan' 'round to watch. Marse George hold de broom 'bout a foot high off
de floor. De one dat jump over it backwards an' never touch de handle,
gwine boss de house, an' if bof of dem jump over without touchin' it,
dey won't gwine be no bossin', dey jus' gwine be 'genial. I jumped fus',
an' you ought to seed me. I sailed right over dat broom stick same as
a cricket, but when Exter jump he done had a big dram an' his feets was
so big an' clumsy dat dey got all tangled up in dat broom an' he fell
head long. Marse George he laugh an' laugh, an' tole Exter he gwine be
bossed 'twell he skeered to speak less'n I tole him to speak. After de
weddin' we went down to de cabin Mis' Betsy done all dressed up, but
Exter couldn' stay no longer den dat night kaze he belonged to Marse
Snipes Durham an' he had to back home. He lef' de nex day for his
plantation, but he come back every Saturday night an' stay 'twell Sunday
night. We had eleven chillun.

TEMPIE HERNDON DURHAM, North Carolina

On Sundays they would let us go to church up at Sassafras Stage, near Bethel. Was the fust church for niggers in these parts. Wasn' no white church; niggers built it an' they had a nigger preacher. 'Couse they wouldn' let us have no services lessen a white man was present. Most times the white preacher would preach, then he would set dere listenin' while the colored preacher preached. That was the law at that time. Couldn' no nigger preacher preach lessen a white man was present, an' they paid the white man what attended the colored services. Niggers had to set an' listen to the white man's sermon, but they didn' want to 'cause they knowed it by heart. Always took his text from Ephesians, the white preacher did, the part what said, "Obey your masters, be good servant."

Can' tell you how many times I done heard that text preached on. They always tell the slaves dat ef he be good an' worked hard fo' his master, dat he would go to heaven, an' dere he gonna live a life of ease. They ain' never tell him he gonna be free in Heaven. You see, they didn' want slaves to start thinkin' 'bout freedom, even in Heaven.

BEVERLY JONES, Virginia

Adeline Cunningham, 1210 Florida St., born 1852, was a slave in Lavaca County, 4½ miles n.e. of Hallettsville. She was a slave of Washington Greenlee Foley and his grandson, John Woods. The Foley plantation consisted of several square leagues, each league containing 4,428.4 acres. Adeline is tall, spare and primly erect, with fiery brown eyes, which snap when she recalls the slave days. The house is somewhat pretentious and well furnished. The day was hot and the granddaughter prepared ice water for her grandmother and the interviewer. House and porch were very clean.
—Unidentified WPA Interviewer

No suh, we never goes to church. Times we sneaks in de woods and prays de Lawd to make us free and times one of de slaves got happy and made a noise dat dey heered at de big house and den de overseer come and whip us 'cause we prayed de Lawd to set us free.

Dey's four or five preachers and de slaves. Iffen days a marriage de preacher has a book. He's gotter keep it hid, 'cause dey's afraid iffen de slaves learns to read dey learns how to run away. One of de slaves runs away and dey ketches him and puts his eyes out. Dey catches anudder slave dat run away and dey hanged him up by de arm. Yassuh, I see dat wid my own eyes; dey holds de slave up by one arm, dey puts a iron on his knee and a iron on his feet and drag 'im down but his feet cain't reach de groun'.

ADELINE CUNNINGHAM, Texas

Adeline Cunningham

Katie Darling

Den dey put de coffin on de oxcart and carried it to de graveyard whar dey jus' had a burial dat day.

De reason dey had slave fun'rals so long atter de burial wuz to have 'em on Sunday or some other time when de crops had been laid by so de other slaves could be on hand.

WILLIS COFER, Georgia

Katie Darling, about 88, was born a slave on the plantation of William McCarty, in the Elysian Fields Road, nine miles south of Marshall, Texas. Katie was a nurse and housegirl in the McCarty household until five years after the end of the Civil War. She then moved to Marshall and married. Her husband and her three children are dead and she is supported by Griffin Williams, a boy she found homeless and reared. They live in a neat three-room shack in Sunny South addition of Marshall, Texas.
—Unidentified WPA Interviewer

When a slave die, massa make the coffin hisself and send a couple niggers to bury the body and say, "Don't be long," and no singin' or prayin' 'lowed, jus' put them in the ground and cover 'em up and hurry on back to that field.

They have dances and parties for the white folks' chillen, but missy say, "Niggers was made to work for white folks," and on Christmas Miss Irene bakes two cakes for the nigger families but she darsn't let missy know 'bout it.

KATIE DARLING, Texas

Wash Wilson, 94, was born a slave of Tom Wilson, in Louisiana, near the Curchita Road. Wash and his family were purchased by Bill Anderson, who brought them to Robertson Co., Texas. Wash lives in Eddy, Texas.
—Unidentified WPA Interviewer

When de niggers go round singin' "Steal Away to Jesus," dat mean dere gwine be a 'ligious meetin' dat night. Dat de sig'fication of a meetin'. De masters 'fore and after freedom didn't like dem 'ligious meetin's, so us natcherly slips off at night, down in de bottoms or somewheres. Sometimes us sing and pray all night.

Dere wasn't no music instruments. Us take pieces a sheep's rib or cow's jaw or a piece iron, with a old kettle, or a hollow gourd and some horsehairs to make de drum. Sometimes dey'd git a piece of tree trunk and hollow it out and stretch a goat's or sheep's skin over it for de drum. Dey'd be one to four foot high and a foot up to six foot 'cross. In gen'ral two niggers play with de fingers or sticks on dis drum. Never seed so many in Texas, but dey made some. Dey'd take de buffalo horn and scrape it out to make de flute. Dat sho' be heared a long ways off. Den dey'd take a mule's jawbone and rattle de stick 'cross its teeth. Dey'd take a barrel and stretch a ox's hide 'cross one end and a man sot 'stride de barrel and beat on dat hide with he hands, and he feet, and iffen he git to feelin' de music in he bones, he'd beat on dat barrel with he head. 'Nother man beat one wooden side with sticks. Us 'longed to de church, all right, but dancin' ain't sinful iffen de foots ain't crossed. Us danced at de arbor meetin's but us sho' didn't have us foots crossed!

WASH WILSON, Texas

Wash Wilson

De overseer woke 'em up 'bout four in de mornin', but I works in de house.
De field workers gits off Thursdays and Saturday evenin's and Sunday.
De reason dey gits off Thursday is dat de massa has some kind of
thought we shouldn't work dat day. Maybe it was 'ligion, I don't know.
We has parties and sings

> Massa sleeps in de feather bed,
> Nigger sleeps on de floor;
> When we'uns gits to Heaven,
> Dey'll be no slaves no mo'.

Den we has de song 'bout dis:

> Rabbit in de briar patch,
> Squirrel in de tree,
> Wish I could go huntin',
> But I ain't free.

> Rooster's in de henhouse,
> Hen's in de patch,
> Love to go shootin',
> But I ain't free.

MILLIE WILLIAMS, Texas

Come Christmas us slaves have de big dinner and eat all day and dance till nex' mornin'. Some de niggers from near plantations git dey passes and come jine us. Course dey a drop egg nog round and candy for de chillen. De white folks have dey big carriage full of visitors and big goin's on dey come to from miles round. Us didn't have no money, but didn't have no place to go to spend it, neither.

YACH STRINGFELLOW, Texas

Sat'day night we would have parties and dance and play ring plays. We had de parties dere in a big double log house. Dey would give us whiskey and wine and cherry brandy, but dere wasn' no shootin' or gamblin'. Dey didn' 'low it. De men and women didn' do like dey do now. If dey had such carryin's on as dey do now, de white folks would have whipped 'em good.

WASH INGRAM, Texas

CHAPTER SEVEN

The Runaway

Whether to try to escape was perhaps the most difficult decision an enslaved African American ever faced. Success meant leaving loved ones behind, most likely forever. Failure meant the torture of the lash at best, death at worst—and the chances of success were not great. Yet every slave probably at least thought of attempting it, so all-consuming was the desire for liberty.

As difficult as it was to contemplate voluntary separation from parents, children, and siblings, the decision was made even more painful by the knowledge that vengeance might be sought against those very people. As he prepared to leave, Francis Federic was overcome by the specter of the treatment his mother would receive: "I could foresee how my master would stand over her with the lash to extort from her my hiding-place. . . . How she would suffer torture on my account, and be distressed that I had left her for ever until we should meet hereafter in heaven I hoped." At the same time, the trauma of losing loved ones often worked as a motivating force for escape attempts, which were frequently precipitated by the imminent threat of separation of families through the ever-present slave trade.

As strong as they were, emotional impediments to flight paled in comparison to the physical ones. "Everything was organized against the slaves' getaway," remembered John Parker,

118

a former fugitive. "The woods were patrolled nightly by constables. . . . Every ford was watched. . . . Once word came from further south that runaways were on the way, the whole countryside turned out . . . to stop the fugitives." Perhaps the most feared obstacles to escape were the dogs kept for tracking down runaways. As Mary Reynolds relates, they were known to eat a person alive before they could be called off.

When John Parker ran, he knew that to his pursuers "I was only a beast of labor in revolt."

Getting caught, however, meant treatment the brutality of which was reserved for human property. After Peter Bruner was caught, he suffered a whipping that nearly killed him. His master "cowhided and cowhided me until the blood stood in pools on the floor . . . I guess he whipped me for about three hours." Bruner kept running. He was not alone.

The yearning to be free was so irrepressible that it was enough to conquer fear and induce persons young and old to endure the severe hardship that was the lot of the fugitive slave. If the dogs did not get them, hunger or the elements often did. The total number of African Americans who escaped southern slavery will never be known; some estimates put it at fifty thousand annually, others at more than a hundred thousand. That does not include the far larger group that never made it to freedom.

These narratives expose some of the persistent myths about the experience of the runaway. The image of fugitive slaves is often closely tied to the institution for aiding their escape that came to be known as the Underground Railroad, usually portrayed as a well-organized conspiracy of sympathetic northern whites. In this respect, Arnold Gragston's words hold important lessons. They show that the enslaved themselves were the clandestine network's most crucial component. Gragston spent four years as a frontline operative in the struggle against slavery—willingly sacrificing his own chance for freedom in order to help others attain that goal. Thomas Cole's fervent hope that he would

encounter Harriet Tubman on his way to Canada demonstrates how much the efforts of African-American freedom fighters served to inspire others to risk it all.

The remembrances of Felix Haywood belie the myth that all runaways headed north and that the only path to freedom was following the North Star. For those enslaved in the Deep South, a southward or westward journey generally represented a more propitious route. Some traveled to New Orleans, hoping to board a ship for England, or simply attempting to disappear in its large population. As Martin Jackson relates, with the onset of the Civil War, joining the Union Army was a sure bet. Thousands liberated themselves by dogging its every step in the heart of the Confederacy, just as at an earlier time some managed to snatch liberty by making use of networks of friends, relatives, and even strangers who kept many a fugitive alive in the vicinity of the plantation they walked away from.

These narratives of escape attest to the perpetual desire to be free that all enslaved African Americans felt. Nothing could more eloquently capture that aspiration than the forceful words of Martin Jackson: "Even with my good treatment, I spent most of my time planning and thinking of running away." The many hundreds of thousands of attempted escapes from bondage embodied the unbreakable spirit of resistance running through the three centuries that slavery lasted on American soil.

Old Solomon gits the
nigger hounds and
takes her trail. They
gits near her and
she grabs a limb and
tries to hist herself
in a tree, but them
dogs grab her and
pull her down.
                    --Mary Reynolds

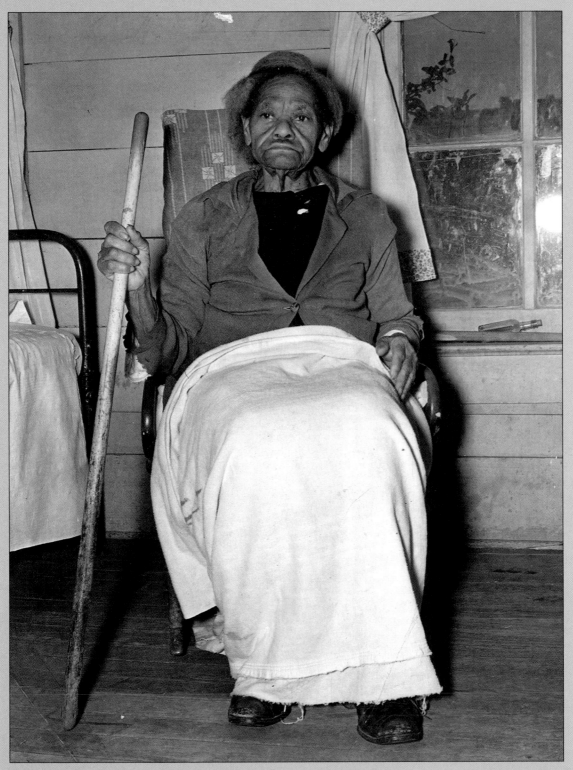

Mary Reynolds

Aunt Cheyney was jus' out of bed with a sucklin' baby one time, and she run away. Some say that was 'nother baby of massa's breedin'. She don't come to the house to nurse her baby, so they misses her and old Solomon gits the nigger hounds and takes her trail. They gits near her and she grabs a limb and tries to hist herself in a tree, but them dogs grab her and pull her down. The men hollers them onto her, and the dogs tore her naker and et the breasts plumb off her body. She got well and lived to be a old woman, but 'nother woman has to suck her baby and she ain't got no sign of breasts no more.

MARY REYNOLDS, Texas

My mammy was de cook. I remember old Master had some purty strict rules and one of 'em was iffen you burnt de bread you had to eat it. One day mammy burnt de bread. She was awful busy and forgot it and it burnt purty bad. She knowed dat old Master would be mad and she'd be punished so she got some grub and her bonnet and she lit out. She hid in de woods and cane brakes for two weeks and dey couldn't find her either. One of de women slipped food out to her. Finally she come home and old Master give her a whipping but he didn't hurt her none. He was glad to git her back. She told us dat she could'a slipped off to de North but she didn't want to leave us children. She was afraid young Master would be mad and sell us and we'd a-had a hard time so she come back. I don't know whether she ever burnt de bread any more or not.

EASTER WELLS, Oklahoma

Arnold Gragston, 97-year-old ex-slave whose early life was spent helping slaves to freedom across the Ohio River, while he, himself, remained in bondage. As he puts it, he guesses he could be called a "conductor" on the underground railway, "only we didn't call it that then. I don't know as we called it anything—we just knew there was a lot of slaves always a-wantin' to get free, and I had to help 'em."
—Martin Richardson, WPA Interviewer

I didn't have no idea of ever gettin' mixed up in any sort of business like that until one special night. I hadn't even thought of rowing across the river myself.

But one night I had gone on another plantation 'courtin', and [an] old woman . . . told me she had a real pretty girl there who wanted to go across the river and would I take her? I was scared and backed out in a hurry. But then I saw the girl, and she was such a pretty little thing, brown-skinned and kinda rosy, and looking as scared as I was feelin', so it wasn't long before I was listenin' to the old woman tell me when to take her and where to leave her on the other side.

I don't know how I ever rowed the boat across the river the current was strong and I was trembling. I couldn't see a thing there in the dark, but I felt that girl's eyes.

It was a long time rowing there in the cold and worryin'. But it was short, too, 'cause as soon as I did get on the other side the big-eyed, brown-skin girl would be gone. Well, pretty soon I saw a tall light and I remembered what the old lady had told me about looking for that light and rowing to it. I did; and when I got up to it, two men reached down and grabbed her; I started tremblin' all over again, and prayin'. Then, one of the men took my arm and I just felt down inside of me that the Lord had got ready for me. "You hungry, Boy?" is what he asked me, and if he hadn't been holdin' me I think I would have fell backward into the river.

That was my first trip; it took me a long time to get over my scared feelin', but I finally did, and I soon found myself goin' back across the river, with two and three people, and sometimes a whole boatload. I got so I used to make three and four trips a month.

I never saw my passengers. I would have to be the "black nights" of the moon when I would carry them.

Those who wanted to stay around that part of Ohio could stay, but didn't many of 'em do it, because there was too much danger that you would be walking along free one night, feel a hand over your mouth, and be back across the river and in slavery again in the morning. And nobody in the world ever got a chance to know as much misery as a slave that had escaped and been caught.

Finally, I saw that I could never do any more good in Mason County, so I decided to take my freedom, too. I had a wife by this time, and one night we quietly slipped across.

I could hear the bell and see the light on Mr. Rankin's place, but the harder I rowed, the farther away it got, and I knew if I didn't make it I'd get killed. But finally, I pulled up by the lighthouse, and went on to my freedom—just a few months before all of the slaves got their's. I didn't stay in Ripley, though; I wasn't taking no chances. I went on to Detroit and still live there with most of 10 children and 31 grandchildren.

The bigger ones don't care so much about hearin' it now, but the little ones never get tired of hearin' how their grandpa brought Emancipation to loads of slaves he could touch and feel, but never could see.

ARNOLD GRAGSTON, Florida

$600 REWARD!

Left the service of the subscriber, near Port Republic, Calvert Co., Md.,

About the 19th of APRIL, 1849

3 NEGRO SLAVES

ONE OF THEM,

HENRY MORSELL

Is an uncommonly large man, being perhaps, six feet two inches high, of a redish copper color, broad across the shoulders, and would weigh over two hundred pounds; he is about 45 years of age, is round shouldered, and somewhat knock-kneed, has a slight impediment in his speech, has a full face, has drank hard and shows the grog blossoms, walks with something of a swinging gait; he has small hands for so large a negro, and usually dresses well.

JIM PARKER,

Is black, about 5 feet 10 inches high, between 25 and 30 years old, has rather a round face, with a fine or thin voice, has a slight stoop in the neck, is rather good-looking, would weigh I suppose about 165 pounds.

BILL HUTTON,

Is dark brown, between 45 and 50 years of age, is some 5 feet 7 or 8 inches high, rather thick set, is generally slow in his motions, and careless in dress.

I will give $600 for the apprehension and detention in jail of the three, so that I get them again; or if taken seperately I will give for the recovery of Henry $250; for Jim I will give $200; and for Bill I will give $150.

I believe they started or will start from the mouth of Patuxent River, in some boat going up or across the Chesapeake Bay.

Port Republic, Calvert Co., Md. 1849   **B. D. BOND.**

☞ For further particulars inquire at No. 8 Bowly's Wharf, Baltimore.

From "The Printing Office," Steam-Power Press, Third Story Sun Iron Building Baltimore.

Even with my good treatment, I spent most of my time planning and thinking of running away. I could have done it easy, but my old father used to say, "No use running from bad to worse, hunting better." Lots of colored boys did escape and joined the Union army, and there are plenty of them drawing a pension today. My father was always counseling me. He said, "Every man has to serve God under his own vine and fig tree."

MARTIN JACKSON, Texas

Jordon Smith, 86, was born in Georgia, a slave of the Widow Hicks. When she died, Jordon, his mother and thirty other slaves were willed to Ab Smith, his owner's nephew, and were later refugeed from Georgia to Anderson Co., Texas. When freed, Jordon worked on a steamboat crew on the Red River until the advent of railroads. For thirty years Jordon worked for the railroad. He is now too feeble to work and lives with his third wife and six children in Marshall, Texas, supported by the latter and his pension of $10.00 a month.
—Unidentified WPA Interviewer

If a nigger ever run off the place and come back, master'd say, "If you'll be a good nigger, I'll not whip you this time." But you couldn't 'lieve that. A nigger run off and stayed in the woods six month. When he come back he's hairy as a cow, 'cause he lived in a cave and come out at night and pilfer round. They put the dogs on him but couldn't cotch him. Fin'ly he come home and master say he won't whip him and Tom was crazy 'nough to 'lieve it. Master say to the cook, "Fix Tom a big dinner," and while Tom's eatin', master stand in the door with a whip and say, "Tom, I's change my mind; you have no business runnin' off and I's gwine take you out jus' like you come into the world."

JORDON SMITH, Texas

Martin Jackson

Thomas Cole was born in Jackson Co., Alabama, on the 8th of August, 1845, a slave of Robert Cole. He ran away in 1861 to join the Union Army. He fought at Chickamauga, under Gen. Rosecran and at Chattanooga, Look Out Mt. and Orchard Knob, under Gen. Thomas. After the war he worked as switchman in Chattanooga until his health failed due to old age. He then came to Texas and lives with his daughter, in Corsicana. Thomas is blind.
—Unidentified WPA Interviewer

I thinks to myself, dat Mr. Anderson, de overseer, he'll give me dat cat-o-nine tails de first chance he gits, but makes up my mind he won't git de chance, 'cause . . . I's gwine north where dere ain't no slaveowners.

When de meat supply runs low, Mr. Sandson sends some slaves to kill a deer or wild hawgs or jes' any kind of game. He never sends me in any dem bunches but I hoped he would and one day he calls me to go and says not to go off de plantation too far, but be sho' bring home some meat. Dis de chance I been wantin', so when we gits to de huntin' ground de leader says to scatter out, and I tells him me and 'nother man goes north and make de circle round de river and meet 'bout sundown. I crosses de river and goes north. I's gwine to de free country, where dey ain't no slaves. I travels all dat day and night up de river and follows de north star. Sev'ral times I thunk de blood houn's am trailin' me and I gits in de big hurry. I's so tired I couldn't hardly move, but I gits in a trot.

I's hopin and prayin' all de time I meets with dat Harriet Tubman woman. She de cullud women what takes slaves to Canada.

THOMAS COLE, Texas

Felix Haywood is a temperamental and whimsical old Negro of San Antonio, Texas, who still sees the sunny side of his 92 years, in spite of his total blindness. He was born and bred a slave in St. Hedwig, Bexar Co., Texas, the son of slave parents bought in Mississippi by his master, William Gudlow. Before and during the Civil War he was a sheep herder and cowpuncher. His autobiography is a colorful contribution, showing the philosophical attitude of the slaves, as well as shedding some light upon the lives of slave owners whose support of the Confederacy was not accompanied by violent hatred of the Union.
—Unidentified WPA Interviewer

Sometimes someone would come 'long and try to get us to run up North and be free. We used to laugh at that. There wasn't no reason to *run* up North. All we had to do was *walk*, but walk *South*, and we'd be free as soon as we crossed the Rio Grande. In Mexico you could be free. They didn't care what color you was, black, white, yellow or blue. Hundreds of slaves did go to Mexico and got on all right. We would hear about 'em and how they was goin' to be Mexicans. They brought up their children to speak only Mexican.

FELIX HAYWOOD, Texas

Felix Haywood

CHAPTER EIGHT

Emancipation

The emancipation of the slaves came with the passage of the Thirteenth Amendment to the Constitution, yet the desire for freedom began when the first Africans landed in Virginia in 1619. As the colonists sought their freedom from the domination of England, the passion for liberty so penetrated society that slaves internalized the belief that liberty would also be theirs to share. The ideals of liberty and equality embodied in the Declaration of Independence were short-lived for the slaves, with only a few being emancipated for service during the Revolutionary War. The concessions the Founding Fathers made to slaveholders sanctioned slavery in the Constitution. It would take eight decades for the nation to extend the promise of freedom to black Americans.

Blacks never gave up on their desire to be free. Gabriel Prosser's attempt at a mass uprising in Henrico County, Virginia, in 1800; Denmark Vesey's efforts to emancipate slaves in Charleston, South Carolina, in 1822; and Nat Turner's insurrection in 1831 in Southampton County, Virginia, were all efforts at self-emancipation. On a lesser scale, but far more widespread, were individual escapes, whether by running away into the forests and swamplands of the South or by traveling on the Underground Railroad.

Black and white abolitionists laid the groundwork for President Lincoln's Emancipation

Proclamation. A small group of agitators, known as abolitionists, believed that slavery was morally wrong. Never accounting for more than one percent of the northern population, they raised the consciousness of society through their protests. In spite of the 1850 Fugitive Slave Law and the 1857 Supreme Court decision in the Dred Scott Case, they persisted in their efforts to rid the nation of slavery.

After Abraham Lincoln was elected president, South Carolina and other southern states seceded from the Union, plunging the nation into a civil war. Yet freeing the slaves was not a presidential wartime objective. President Lincoln wrote in 1862, "My paramount object in this struggle is to save the Union, and is not either to save or destroy slavery. If I could save the Union without freeing any slave, I would do it; and if I could save it by freeing some and leaving others alone, I would also do that."

Abolitionists such as Frederick Douglass, Susan B. Anthony, Angelina Grimke Weld, and Wendell Phillips continued to be strong spokespersons for emancipation, and never wavered in their belief that the war was being fought for freedom of the slaves. They were instrumental in getting the North to recognize the injustice and the inconsistency of slavery in a democracy dedicated to "liberty and justice for all." Even so, President Lincoln and Congress were more cautious in their approach until it became apparent that freeing the slaves might aid in winning the war.

In 1862 in Virginia and other areas, Union forces had suffered several military reverses. The governments of Great Britain and France considered recognizing the Confederate States of America. If the war was to free the slaves, England was unlikely to side with the Confederates. Suddenly, turning the Civil War into a crusade against slavery began to make political sense.

Lincoln wrote the Emancipation Proclamation in September 1862 but delayed issuing it until the Army of the Potomac won a victory. The victory came at the Battle of Antietam in Maryland on September 17, 1862. The reluctant emancipator tried to establish a policy of "compensated emancipation" to appease citizens in the border states. Slavery was abolished with compensation in the District of Columbia. Army officers no longer returned fugitive slaves to their owners. Yet when Lincoln finally announced his preliminary proclamation on September 22, 1862, he chose to phrase the Emancipation Proclamation in a manner least likely to offend slaveholders in border states. The proclamation declared that "all persons held as slaves within any State or designated part of a State the people whereof shall then be in rebellion against the United States, shall be then, thenceforward, and forever free." These states included Maryland, Delaware, Missouri, and Kentucky. The proclamation applied to states and areas not under federal control and thus where it could not be enforced. The Commander-in-Chief declared

the Emancipation Proclamation effective January 1, 1863.

Blacks had not waited for Lincoln to provide their Day of Jubilee. They had never given up the hope or the desire for freedom. The seeds of the American Revolution had been firmly planted in them and their descendants. This craving for freedom was reflected in their cosmology, as can be seen in their spirituals. Freedom was escape from punishment and was about getting their just rewards in an unjust land.

While restrictions were an inherent part of slavery, movement was essential to freedom. The slaves had to move beyond the plantations to test their freedom. This "movement" appeared to white southerners as if blacks were trying to avoid what they needed them most

to do, work the land. Southerners were determined to regain economic and political control over the South. While slavery was "ended," and blacks were guaranteed the rights of citizens, a series of events—violence, intimidation, withdrawal of federal troops, adverse decisions of the Supreme Court—contributed to the denial of freedom to the freedmen. By the time of the Federal Writers Project of the 1930s and the recording of the "Slave Narratives," southern whites had long cemented their control of the South. Rayford Logan described the period as the "nadir." Many felt like Sarah Ashley of Texas as she summarized her feelings in her narrative: "Now I's all alone and thinks of dem old times what was so bad, and I's ready for de Lawd to call me."

"Well dis de fourth day
of June, and dis is 1865,
and I want you all to
'member de date, 'cause
you allus going 'member
de day. Today you is
free. Jest lak I is, and
Mr. Saunders and your
Mistress and all us white
people," de man say.

--Katie Rowe

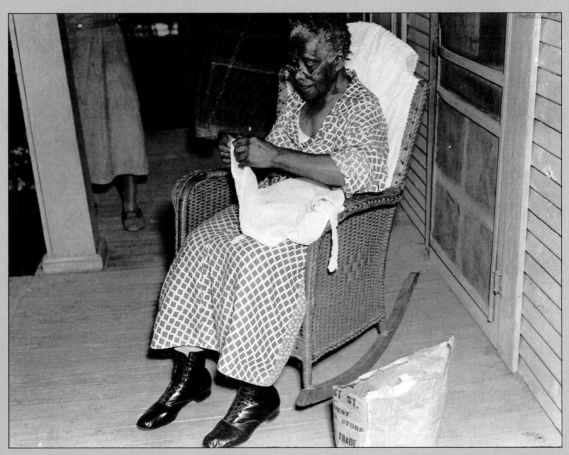

Katie Rowe

Old Master live in town and jest had de overseer on de place, but iffen he had lived out dar hisself I speck it been as bad, 'cause he was a hard driver his own self.

He git biling mad when de Yankees have dat big battle at Pea Ridge and scatter de 'Federates all down through our country all bleeding and tied up and hungry, and he jest mount on his hoss and ride out to de plantation whar we all hoeing corn. He ride up and tell old man Saunders—dat de overseer—to bunch us all up round de lead row man—dat my own uncle Sandy—and den he tell us de law!

"You niggers been seeing de 'Federate soldiers coming by here looking purty raggedy and hurt and wore out," he say, "but dat no sign dey licked! Dem Yankees ain't gwine git dis fur, but iffen dey do you all ain't gwine git free by 'em, 'cause I gwine free you befo' dat. When dey git here dey going find you already free, 'cause I gwine line you up on de bank of Bois d'Arc Creek and free you wid my shotgun! Anybody miss jest one lick wid de hoe, or one step in de line, or one clap of dat bell, or one toot of de horn, and he gwine be free and talking to de debil long befo' he ever see a pair of blue britches!"

I never forget de day we was set free! Dat morning we all go to de cotton field early, and den a house nigger come out from old Mistress on a hoss and say she want de overseer to come into town, and he leave and go in. After while de old horn blow up at de overseer's house, and we all stop and listen, 'cause it de wrong time of day for de horn.

We start chopping again, and dar go de horn again. De lead row nigger holler "Hold up!" And we all stop again. "We better go on in. Dat our horn," he holler at de head nigger, and de head nigger think so too, but he say he afraid we catch de devil from de overseer iffen we quit widout him dar, and de lead row man say maybe he back from town and blowing de horn hisself, so we line up and go in.

Setting on de gallery in a hide-bottom chair was a man we never see before. He had on a big broad black hat lak de Yankees wore but it din't have no yaller string on it lak most de Yankees had, and he was in store clothes dat wasn't homespun or jeans, and dey was black. His hair was plumb gray and so was his beard, and it come way down here on his chest, but he didn't look lak he was very old, 'cause his face was kind of fleshy and healthy looking. I think we all been sold off in a bunch, and I notice some kind of smiling, and I think they sho' glad of it.

De man say, "You darkies know what dey dis is?" He talk kind, and smile. We all don't know of course, and we jest stand dar and grin. Pretty soon he ask again and de head man say, No, we don't know. "Well dis de fourth day of June, and dis is 1865, and I want you all to 'member de date, 'cause you allus going 'member de day. Today you is free. Jest lak I is, and Mr. Saunders and your Mistress and all us white people," de man say.

"I come to tell you," he say, "and I wants to be sho' you all understand, 'cause you don't have to git up and go by de horn no more. You is your own bosses now, and you don't have to have no passes to go and come." We never did have no passes, nohow, but we knowed lots of other niggers on other plantations got 'em.

"I wants to bless you and hope you always is happy, and tell you got all de right and lief dat any white people got," de man say, and den he git on his hoss and ride off.

KATIE ROWE, Oklahoma

Wash Ingram

Master Ingram had 350 slaves when de war was over but he didn' turn us
loose till a year after surrender. He told us dat de gov'ment goin' to
give us 40 acres of land and a pair of mules, but we didn't git nothin'.

WASH INGRAM, Texas

Julia Williams, born in Wine-
park, Chesterfield County near
Richmond, Virginia. Her age is
estimated close to 100 years.
A little more or a little less, it
is not known for sure.

Her memory is becoming
faded. She could remember her
mothers name was Katharine

but her father died when she
was very small and she remembers not his name.

Julia had three sisters,
Charlotte, Rose and Emaline
Mack. The last names of the
first two, Charlotte and Rose
she could not recall.

As her memory is becoming
faded, her thoughts wander
from one thing to another and
her speech is not very plain,
the following is what I heard
and understood during the
interview.

—Forest H. Lees,
WPA Interviewer

After de War de had to pick their own livin' and seek homes.

Shuah, deh expected de 40 acres of lan' and mules, but deh had to
work foh dem.

Shuah, deh got path of de lan but de shuah had to work foh it.

After de war deh had no place to stay and den deh went to so many
diffrunt places. Some of dem today don't have settled places to live.

Yes, some of de slaves were force to stay on de plantation. I see how
some had to live. They had homes for awhile but when deh weren't
able to pay dere rent cause deh weren't paid, deh were thrown out of
dere houses.

When I were free, one morning I seed the mistress and she ask me
would I stay with her a couple years. I say, "No, I gonna find mah
people an go dere." Anyway, she had a young mister, a son, an he was
mean to de slaves. I nebber lak him.

JULIA WILLIAMS, Ohio

Walter Calloway lives alone half a block off Avenue F, the thoroughfare on the southside of Birmingham on which live many of the leaders in the Negro life of the city. For his eighty-nine years he was apparently vigorous except for temporary illness. A glance at the interior of his cabin disclosed the fact that it was scrupulously neat and quite orderly in arrangement, a characteristic of a great many ex-slaves. As he sat in the sunshine on his tiny front porch, his greeting was: "Come in, white folks. You ain't no doctor is you?"

To a negative reply, he explained as he continued, "Fo' de las' past twenty-five years I been keepin' right on, wukkin' for de city in de street department. 'Bout two mont's ago dis mis'ry attackted me an' don't 'pear lak nothin' dem doctors gimme do no good. De preacher he come to see me dis mornin' an' he say he know a white gemman doctor, what he gwine to sen' him to see me. I sho' wants to git well ag'in pow'ful bad, but mebby I done live long 'nuff an' my time 'bout come."
—W. F. Jordan, WPA Interviewer

But lawdy, Cap'n, we ain't neber been what I calls free. 'Cose ole marster didn' own us no mo', an' all de folks soon scatter all ober, but iffen dey all lak me dey still hafter wuk jes' as hard, an some times hab less dan we useter hab when we stay on Marse John's plantation.

WALTER CALLOWAY, Alabama

When ole marster comes down in de cotton patch to tell us 'bout bein' free, he say, "I hates to tell you but I knows I's got to, you is free, jes' as free as me or anybody else whats white." We didn' hardly know what he means. We jes' sort of huddle 'round together like scared rabbits, but after we knowed what he mean, didn' many of us go, 'cause we didn' know where to of went.

JENNY PROCTOR, Texas

Jenny Proctor

I was glad when de war stopped kaze den me an' Exter could be together all de time 'stead of Saturday an' Sunday. After we was free we lived right on at Marse George's plantation a long time. We rented de lan' for a fo'th of what we made, den after while be bought a farm. We paid three hundred dollars we done saved. We had a hoss, a steer, a cow an' two pigs, 'sides some chickens an' fo' geese. Mis' Betsy went up in de attic an' give us a bed an' bed tick; she give us enough goose feathers to make two pillows, den she give us a table an' some chairs. She give us some dishes too. Marse George give Exter a bushel of seed cawn an some seed wheat, den he tole him to go down to de barn an' get a bag of cotton seed. We got all dis den we hitched up de wagon an' th'owed in de passel of chillun an' moved to our new farm, an' de chillun was put to work in de fiel'; dey growed up in de fiel' kaze dey was put to work time dey could walk good.

TEMPIE HERNDON DURHAM, North Carolina

We wuz glad ter be free, an' lemmie tell yo', we shore cussed ole marster out 'fore we left dar; den we comed ter Raleigh. I'se always been a farmer an' I'se made right good. I lak de white folkses an' dey laks me but I'll tell yo' Miss, I'd ruther be a nigger any day dan to be lak my ole white folks wuz.

CHARLIE CRUMP, North Carolina

The end of the war, it com jus' like that—like you snap your fingers.

Hallelujah broke out—

> Abe Lincoln freed the nigger
> With the gun and the trigger;
> And I ain't goin' to get whipped any more.
> I got my ticket,
> Leavin' the thicket,
> And I'm a-headin' for the Golden Shore!

Soldiers, all of a sudden, was everywhere—comin' in bunches, crossin' and walkin' and ridin'. Everyone was a-singin'. We was all walkin' on golden clouds. Hallelujah!

> Union forever,
> Hurrah, boys, hurrah!
> Although I may be poor,
> I'll never be a slave—
> Shoutin' the battle cry of freedom.

Everybody went wild. We all felt like heroes and nobody had made us that way but ourselves. We was free. Just like that, we was free. It didn't seem to make the whites mad, either. They went right on giving us food just the same. Nobody took our homes away, but right off colored folks started on the move. They seemed to want to get closer to freedom, so they'd know what it was—like it was a place or a city.

FELIX HAYWOOD, Texas

When de boss man told us freedom was come he didn't like it, but he give all us de bale of cotton and some corn. He ask us to stay and he'p with de crop but we'uns so glad to git 'way dat nobody stays. I got 'bout fifty dollars for de cotton and den I lends it to a nigger what never pays me back yit. Den I got no place to go, so I cooks for a white man name' Dick Cole. He sposen give me $5.00 de month but he never paid me no money. He'd give me eats and clothes, 'cause he has de little store.

Now, I's all alone and thinks of dem old times what was so bad, and I's ready for de Lawd to call me.

SARAH ASHLEY, Texas

De happies' time o' my life wuz when Cap'n Tipton, a Yankee soljer cumed an' tol' us de wah wuz ober an' we wuz free. Cap'n Tipton sez, "Youse de boys we dun dis foah". We shure didn't lose no time gittin' 'way; no man.

We went to Lewisburg an' den up to Cha'leston by wagon an' den tuk de guvment boat, *Genrul Crooks*, an' it brung us heah to Gallipolis in 1865. Dat Ohio shoah shure looked prutty.

I'se shure thankful to Mr. Lincoln foah whut he dun foah us folks, but dat Jeff Davis, well I ain't sayin' whut I'se thinkin'.

de is jes like de worl', der is lots o' good an' lots o' bad in it.

JAMES CAMPBELL, Ohio

I remember so well how the
roads was full of folks
walking and walking along
when the niggers were
freed. Didn't know where
they was going. Just going
to see about something else
somewhere else. Meet a body
in the road and they ask,
    "Where you going?"
    "Don't know."
    "What you going to do?"
    "Don't know."
And then I begins to
think and to know I never
had to be a slave no more.
                    --Robert Falls

CONTRIBUTING AUTHORS

LONNIE G. BUNCH is the President of the Chicago Historical Society and has served as Associate Director for Curatorial Affairs and Senior Curator of Political History at the National Museum of American History. Bunch was also the Founding Curator of the California African-American Museum in Los Angeles. Bunch has curated numerous museum exhibitions and has published extensively on African-American history. He holds undergraduate and graduate degrees in American and African-American History from the American University and is an adjunct professor of Museum Studies at George Washington University and a documentary filmmaker.

SPENCER R. CREW is the Executive Director and CEO of the National Underground Railroad Freedom Center. For twenty years before that he worked at the Smithsonian Institution's National Museum of American History. From 1992 until 2001 he was the director of that museum. He served as curator for the exhibition "Field to Factory: Afro-American Migration 1915–1940" and co-curator for "The American Presidency: A Glorious Burden." He has published on these topics and others related to African-American history and public history. He received his undergraduate degree from Brown University and his graduate degrees from Rutgers University.

DR. REX M. ELLIS is Vice President of the Historic Area at the Colonial Williamsburg Foundation. Prior to his current position, Ellis was Curator and Chair of the Division of Cultural History at the National Museum of American History in Washington, D.C. His presentations, lectures, workshops, and consultancies focus on public programming, diversity, and interpretation. His disciplinary interests include the spoken word and early American History, with special emphasis on slavery.

JOHN E. FLEMING, author and historian, is Vice President of Museums at Cincinnati Museum Center. He received his B.A. from Berea College and his M.A. and Ph.D. from Howard University in Washington, D.C. He was the first director for the National Underground Railroad Freedom Center and the National Afro-American Museum at Wilberforce, Ohio. He was President of the Ohio Museums Association and the Association of African-American Museums. He has written four books and forty-two articles. He is married to Barbara Fleming, a psychologist and mystery writer. They have two daughters.

HENRY LOUIS GATES, JR., is the chair of Harvard's Afro-American Studies Department. Instrumental in changing the literary canon, he has edited many long-lost works, including *The Bondwoman's Narrative* and *Our Nig*, was the co-editor of *The Norton Anthology of African-American Literature*, and has written several major critical texts including *The African-American Century: How Black America Has Shaped Our Country*. His work has helped to broaden the definitions of both American and African-American literature.

CYNTHIA GOODMAN is a museum director, curator, author, educator, and multimedia producer. Currently she is organizing the exhibition "Unchained Memories" as Guest Curator for the National Underground Railroad Freedom Center in Cincinnati. Dr. Goodman received her Ph.D. in Art History from the University of Pennsylvania. She has written numerous books, exhibition catalogs, and magazine articles and has organized and installed exhibitions for institutions including The Metropolitan Museum of Art and the Whitney Museum of American Art in New York, Centre Georges Pompidou in Paris, and the National Building Museum in Washington, D.C. Dr. Goodman also lectures at museums, universities, and conferences.

KEITH GRIFFLER is Assistant Professor of African-American History at the University of Cincinnati. He is author of *What Price Alliance: Black Radicals Confront White Labor, 1918–1938*. He is currently completing his second book, *Wade in the Water: The Underground Railroad and African American Freedom in the Ohio Valley*, and is co-producer of a public television documentary on that subject.

WALTER B. HILL, JR., is a Senior Archivist and Subject Area Specialist at the National Archives and Records Administration, specializing in records relative to the documentation of African Americans in federal records. He received his Ph.D. in American History from the University of Maryland. Since 1984 he has been an Adjunct Professor in the Afro-American Studies Department at Howard University. He has published articles in the area of archives and history with specific focus on Afro-American life, history, and culture and has participated in several historical documentaries on African Americans. He is a board member of the Executive Council of the Association for the Study of Afro-American History as well as a commissioner on the Maryland State Commission for Afro-American Life and Culture and Chief Historian for the African American Civil War Memorial.

DR. ORLOFF MILLER is the Director of the Freedom Stations Program and Interim Director of Research Programs at the National Underground Railroad Freedom Center. Orloff is a historical archaeologist, community historian, and preservation planner and has documented literally hundreds of archaeology sites, architectural resources, and community memories in fourteen states and in Northern Ireland. He came to these field skills after receiving his B.A. in Anthropology at the Colorado College and his M.A. and Ph.D. in American Civilization at the University of Pennsylvania.

DELORES WALTERS holds a Ph.D. in Anthropology and is a community education specialist at the National Underground Railroad Freedom Center in Cincinnati. She is also a faculty member in the Sociology, Anthropology, and Philosophy department and Institute for Freedom Studies at Northern Kentucky University. Her teaching both in the classroom and in the community involves researching the Underground Railroad in the Ohio-Kentucky borderlands. Previously, she facilitated collaborations on Underground Railroad research involving the Madison County Freedom Trail Commission and Colgate University in upstate New York.

SUGGESTED READING

BOOKS

Berlin, Ira. *Many Thousands Gone: The First Two Centuries of Slavery in North America.* Cambridge: Harvard University Press, 2000.

Berlin, Ira, Marc Favreau, and Steven F. Miller, eds. *Remembering Slavery: African Americans Talk About Their Personal Experiences of Slavery and Freedom.* New York: The New Press, 1998.

Blassingame, John W. *The Slave Community: Plantation Life in the Antebellum South.* New York: Oxford University Press, 1979.

Blockson, Charles L., with Ron Fry. *Black Genealogy: How to Discover Your Own Family's Roots and Trace Your Ancestors Back Through an Eventful Past, Even to a Specific African Kingdom.* Baltimore: Black Classic Press, 1977.

Botkin, A., ed. *Lay My Burden Down: A Folk History of Slavery.* Chicago: University of Chicago Press, 1945.

Bruner, Carrie, ed. *A Slave's Adventures Toward Freedom; No Fiction, But the True Story of a Struggle.* Oxford, OH: s.n., 1918.

Campbell, Edward D. C., Jr., and Kym S. Rice, eds. *Before Freedom Came: African-American Life in the Antebellum South.* Richmond: University Press of Virginia, 1991.

Douglass, Frederick. *My Bondage and My Freedom.* Mineola, NY: Dover Publications, 1969.

Ferguson, Leland. *Uncommon Ground: Archaeology and Early African America, 1650–1800.* Washington, D.C.: Smithsonian Press, 1992.

Franklin, John Hope. *From Slavery to Freedom: A History of the African Americans,* 7th Edition. New York: Alfred A. Knopf, 1994.

Franklin, John Hope, and Alfred Moss, Jr. *From Slavery to Freedom: A History of African Americans,* 8th edition, vol. one. New York: McGraw-Hill, 2000.

Franklin, John Hope, and Loren Schweninger. *Runaway Slaves: Rebels on the Plantation.* New York: Oxford University Press, 2000.

Gaspar, David Barry, and Darlene Clark Hine, eds. *More Than Chattel: Black Women and Slavery in the Americas.* Urbana: Indiana University Press, 1996.

Gates, Henry Louis, Jr., and Nellie Y. McKay. *The Norton Anthology: African American Literature.* New York: W.W. Norton and Company, 1997.

Genovese, Eugene D. *Roll, Jordan, Roll: The World the Slaves Made.* New York: Vintage Books, 1976.

Gutman, Herbert. *The Black Family in Slavery and Freedom.* New York: Pantheon Press, 1976.

Jacobs, Harriet. *Incidents in the Life of a Slave Girl, Written by Herself.* Cambridge: Harvard University Press, 2001.

Joyner, Charles. *Down by the Riverside: A South Carolina Slave Community.* Urbana: University of Illinois Press, 1984.

Lee, Rev. Charles, ed. *Slave Life in Virginia and Kentucky; or, Fifty Years of Slavery in the Southern States of America.* London: Wertheim, Macintosh, and Hunt, 1863.

Logan, Rayford W. *The Betrayal of the Negro, from Rutherford B. Hayes to Woodrow Wilson.* New York: Da Capo Press, 1965.

McPherson, James M. *Battle Cry of Freedom: The Civil War Era.* New York: Oxford University Press, 1988.

Morgan, Phillip D. *Slave Counterpoint: Black Culture in the Eighteenth-Century Chesapeake & Lowcountry.* Chapel Hill: University of North Carolina Press, 1998.

Oliver, James, and Lois E. Horton. *Hard Road to Freedom: The Story of African America.* New Brunswick, NJ: Rutgers University Press, 2001.

Owens, Howard. *This Species of Property: Slave Life and Culture in the Old South.* New York: Oxford University Press, 1976.

Parker, John P. *His Promised Land: The Autobiography of John P. Parker, Former Slave, and Conductor on the Underground Railroad.* Stuart Seely Sprague, ed. New York: W.W. Norton and Company, 1996.

Phillips, Ulrich B. *Life and Labor in the Old South.* New York: Little, Brown and Company, 1929.

Rawick, George P., et al., eds. *The American Slave: A Composite Autobiography.* Westport, CT: Greenwood Press, 1972–79.

Robinson, Randall. *The Debt: What America Owes to Blacks.* New York: Dutton, 2000.

Runyon, Randolph Paul. *Delia Webster and the Underground Railroad.* Lexington: The University Press of Kentucky, 1996.

St. George, Robert Blair, ed. *Material Life in America 1600–1860.* Boston: Northeastern University Press, 1988.

Sernett, Milton C. *North Star Country: Upstate New York and the Crusade for African American Freedom.* Syracuse, NY: Syracuse University Press, 2002.

Singleton, Theresa, ed. *The Archaeology of Slavery and Plantation Life.* New York: Academic Press, 1977.

Stampp, Kenneth M. *The Peculiar Institution: Slavery in the Ante-Bellum South.* New York: Vintage Books, 1956.

Stauffer, John. *The Black Hearts of Men: Radical Abolitionists and the Transformation of Race.* Cambridge: Harvard University Press, 2002.

Thomas, Hugh. *The Slave Trade.* New York: Simon and Schuster, 1997.

Tobin, Jacqueline L., and Raymond G. Dobard. *Hidden in Plain View: A Secret Story of Quilts and the Underground Railroad.* New York: Anchor Books, 1999.

Vlach, John Michael. *Back of the Big House: The Architecture of Plantation Slavery.* Chapel Hill: University of North Carolina Press, 1993.

Wade, Richard C. *Slavery in Cities: The South 1820–1860.* London: Oxford University Press, 1964.

Weisenberger, Steven. *Modern Medea: A Family Story of Slavery and Child Murder from the Old South.* New York: Hill and Wang, 1998.

Yetman, Norman, ed. *Voices from Slavery: 100 Authentic Slave Narratives.* Mineola, NY: Dover Publications, 1972.

WEBSITES

The Library of Congress, Born in Slavery Project: Slave Narratives from the Federal Writers' Project, 1936–38

http://memory.loc.gov/ammem/snhtml/snhome.html

The Library of Congress, "A Florida Treasure Hunt" by Stetson Kennedy

http://memory.loc.gov/ammem/flwpahtml

Stetson Kennedy

www.stetson.kennedy.com

NARRATIVES SOURCE LIST

Federal Writers' Project, United States Work Progress Administration (USWPA); Manuscript Division, Library of Congress

Alabama Narratives, Volume 1
Walter Calloway
Laura Clark
William Colbert
Delia Garlic
Lucindy Lawrence Jurdon
Tom McAlpin
Mingo White

Arkansas Narratives, Volume 2, Part 5
Mary Estes Peters

Florida Narratives, Volume 3
Arnold Gragston

Georgia Narratives, Volume 4
Part 1	Part 2
Marshal Butler	Shang Harris
Willis Cofer	

Indiana Narratives, Volume 5
John W. Fields

Missouri Narratives, Volume 10
Sarah Frances Shaw Graves

North Carolina Narratives, Volume 11
Part 1	Part 2
Louisa Adams	Fannie Moore
W. L. Bost	
Charlie Crump	
Tempie Herndon Durham	
Sarah Gudger	

Ohio Narratives, Volume 12
James Campbell
Julia Williams

Oklahoma Narratives, Volume 13
Octavia George
Katie Rowe
Easter Wells
Charley Williams

South Carolina Narratives, Volume 14
Part 1	Part 4
Henry Coleman	Rosa Starke

Tennessee Narratives, Volume 15
Robert Falls

Texas Narratives, Volume 16
Part 1	Part 2
Sarah Ashley	James Green
Francis Black	Felix Haywood
Cato Carter	Wash Ingram
Thomas Cole	Carter J. Jackson
Adeline Cunningham	Martin Jackson
Katie Darling	Richard Jackson

Part 3	Part 4
Charley Mitchell	Jordan Smith
William Moore	Yach Stringfellow
Jenny Proctor	Millie Williams
Mary Reynolds	Rose Williams
	Wash Wilson

Virginia Narratives, Volume 17
Fannie Berry
Elizabeth Sparks

American Slave, Supplemental Series 2, Volume 7
Jack and Rosa Maddox

Virginia Federal Writers' Project Hampton University Archives
Beverly Jones
Rev. Ishrael Massie

ACKNOWLEDGMENTS

The National Underground Railroad Freedom Center would like to thank the following for their contributions to this project:

Neither this publication nor the exhibition would have been possible without the extraordinary generosity and vision of AOL Time Warner, which has been not only a sponsor but also a partner, enthusiastically making so many of the corporation's assets available to us. We would like to express our special thanks to Virginia McEnerney, vice president of corporate relations, for the leadership position she has assumed in directing this project, as well as to Jennifer Mooney, vice president of marketing, Time Warner Cable, Cincinnati, who has been involved in all aspects of making this exhibition a reality. Bonnie Hathaway has also helped give our project a national scope.

We are deeply grateful to Zachary Morfogen, who has helped nurture and shape this project from the beginning and continues to remain a key contributor to all aspects of this publication and exhibition.

A very special thanks goes to Jackie Glover, producer of the film, without whose editorial contribution, knowledge, and passion this book could not have been created. Executive producer Donna Brown Guillaume, co-producer and editor Juliet Weber, and director Ed Bell should also be acknowledged for their dedicated work on the documentary.

We would also like to thank Michael Sand, executive editor, and Karyn Gerhard, editor, at Bulfinch Press, both of whom have been an extraordinary pleasure to work with despite the challenges of our production schedule. Sand's vision and dedication have been the motivating forces behind making this publication possible. We are profoundly thankful as well to the scholars who wrote the eight chapter essays: Lonnie G. Bunch, the Chicago Historical Society; Spencer Crew, National Underground Railroad Freedom Center; Rex Ellis, Colonial Williamsburg Foundation; John Fleming, Cincinnati Museum Center; Keith Griffler, University of Cincinnati; Walter Hill, National Archives; Orloff Miller, National Underground Railroad Freedom Center; Delores Walters, Northern Kentucky University. All these authors produced excellent introductions to the often difficult subject matter in their respective sections of this publication in record time.

We are deeply indebted to Stetson Kennedy for sharing his vivid memories of his WPA experience as well as offering to let us review his personal archives. Adrienne Cannon, in charge of the African-American material in the Library of Congress Manuscripts Division under whose jurisdiction the "Slave Narratives" are archived, was an invaluable help, not only with the "Slave Narratives" but also with numerous other materials about which we otherwise might not have known. Steve Rutt also deserves thanks for his technical assistance with many aspects of presenting our research in a digital format. At the Freedom Center, Darlene Barnes has been a great and enthusiastic assistant with our research, and Kimberley de Stefano coordinated many details.

At HBO, we are indebted to our chairman and CEO, Chris Albrecht, the film's executive producer, Sheila Nevins, for having the extraordinary vision to make this film, and senior producer Lisa Heller, for her commitment to maximizing its impact. Richard Plepler, executive vice president, should also be acknowledged for his constant support and encouragement for important documentary programming at HBO. The chance to shape both a publication and an exhibition to complement and expand upon their inspiring achievement in film has been a privilege. They have also generously shared their research knowledge about the "Slave Narratives" with us. Dan Sacher, Sara Bernstein, Peter Megler, Bree Conover, and Atiyah Muhammad have been invaluable colleagues in our mutual quest for the appropriate materials to complement our respective tasks, and Cindy Matero, director of marketing, has eagerly assisted with our education component.

PICTURE CREDITS

Avery Center: jacket: bottom row left; **Chicago Historical Society**: 134–5; **Florida State Archives**: 6, 49, 89, jacket: center row middle; **Greg French**: 38; **The J. Paul Getty Museum, Los Angeles**: 4–5; **Historic Arkansas Museum**: jacket: center row left; **Illinois State Historical Library**: 102–3, 109 (detail); **Library of Congress**: 25, 29, 33, 35, 41, 44, 51, 53, 54–5, 59, 63, 65, 68–9, 71, 79, 80, 83, 85, 91, 93, 95, 97, 107, 111, 112, 115, 117, 118–19, 120, 123, 129, 130, 133, 137, 139, 142, 145, 146–7, jacket: top row all, bottom row right; **Louisiana State Museum**: 36–7; **Menil Collection Foundation**: 86–7; **Missouri Historical Society**: 22; **National Archives**: 100; **Collection of The New-York Historical Society**: 57, 66–7, 74, jacket: center row right; **New York Public Library**: jacket: bottom row center; **North Wind Picture Archives**: 104; **Ohio Historical Society**: 151; **Schomburg Research Center**: 27; **University of Kentucky**: 30; **University of North Carolina Chapel Hill**: 18, 20–1, 46–7; **Wisconsin Historical Society**: 127.

THE DOCUMENTARY

Unchained Memories: Readings from the Slave Narratives is an HBO documentary special, produced in association with the Library of Congress, home of the Slave Narratives Collection. The documentary debuts exclusively on HBO in February 2003, to commemorate Black History Month, and is the centerpiece of an extensive HBO outreach and educational project targeting museums, libraries, colleges, and high schools across the country. In association with the National Underground Freedom Center, the traveling exhibition and this companion book from Bulfinch Press were also developed in conjunction with the broadcast.

THE EXHIBITION

The exhibition organized by the National Underground Railroad Freedom Center, Cincinnati, Ohio, to complement and expand upon the HBO documentary *Unchained Memories* begins its national museum tour in spring 2003 and will be shown at the National Underground Railroad Freedom Center in the summer of 2004. This exhibition and its national tour are presented courtesy of AOL Time Warner.

Organized under the direction of Dr. Cynthia Goodman, Guest Curator, the exhibition is an interactive multimedia presentation containing archival materials as well as audio recordings of former slaves previously available only at the Library of Congress, a registry for visitors to record information about relatives or others who were former slaves, information about the Underground Railroad, and curriculum materials developed by HBO and the National Underground Railroad Freedom Center. The exhibition will also include approximately sixty-five photos from the Library of Congress Archives with accompanying texts. Special viewing areas will continuously run the HBO film and a video presentation of WPA former slave interviewer Stetson Kennedy amplified by materials from his personal archival collection.

It Ain't De Same

(Photo)

    Lucindy Lawrence Jurdon bustled feverishly about her tiny
Lee County cabin when she learned her picture was "goin' to be tuk."
She got out her old spinning wheel; sat down before it and beamed.
Her daughter coming in from the field, exclaimed: "Ma, I done tol'
you dis lady was comin' to see you; an' you wouldn't believe me."

    After she had posed, she seated herself to tell about slavery
days. Her oldest grandson was sick in the next room with pneumonia;
the cabin was stuffy and bare.

    Lucindy said:

    "Honey, I was borned in Macon, Georgy, on de twenty-eighth day
of some month or other; I can't 'member which. But de year was 1858.

    "My pappy an' mammy, Emanuel and Patsy Lawrence, come from Jas-
per County, Georgy. I had a sister named Jennie an' a brother named
Phillip, but I was de oldest.

    "Ol' Marster had 'bout three or four hundred acres on his plan-
tation. His name was Marster LeRoy Lawrence, and he shorely was good
to all us niggers. His daddy was Mr. Billy Lawrence; an' de marster
had four chilluns.

    "Us lived in a two-room log house wid a lean-to next it. Us
was well off in dem times, but us didn't have sense enough to know
it. I 'members dat us always had plenty of good victuals.

    "Honey, us had meat broiled on hot rocks, roasted 'taters, ash-
cake an sech. On Sunday us had ash-cake cooked in collard leaves;
an' beef was served us when de killin' time come. Marster always
gived de niggers plenty to eat.

    "I can sit here an' picture dat house of marster's; a big, six-